the GREAT BIG SCOTTISH FUN BOOK

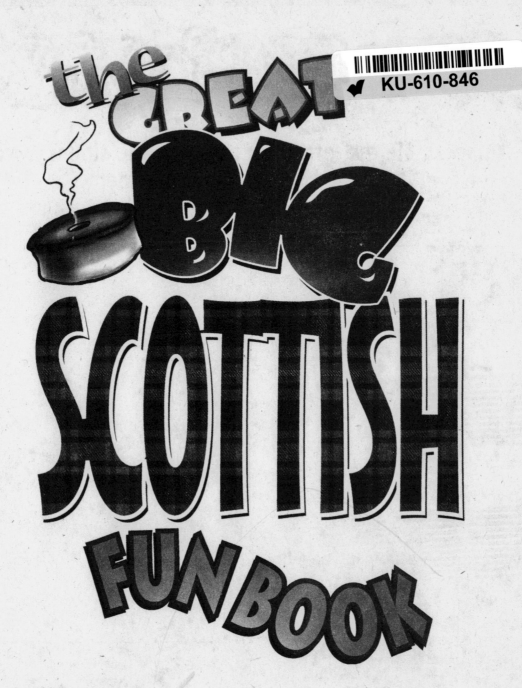

Words, Words, Words

Unscramble the letters in the boxes to find a word associated with Scottish scenery.

U	N	O
A	N	S
M	I	T

When you have found the word, see how many other words of three letter or more you can make from it. The letter appearing in the black box must appear in all your words.

BEE SILLY!

A

B

C

D

E

F

G

H

E

I

J

K

Only two of these bees are exactly alike. Can you spot them?

Smiffy went to the dentist to get wisdom teeth put in.

When Smiffy went hitch-hiking, he left early to avoid the traffic.

Smiffy was listening to the match last night and burnt his ear.

WHAT'S ROUND, WHITE AND GIGGLES?
A tickled onion.

WHAT DO YOU GET WHEN YOU CROSS A HYENA WITH A BEEF CUBE?
A laughing stock.

THE BIG BREAKFAST!

CHIEF'S PORRIDGE, THE NOO -

Hamish has asked all his friends round for breakfast. Complete the empty boxes to find out all they had to eat - apart from porridge!

MAPPED OUT!

The place names in this map of mainland Scotland are all in the wrong places. Can you put it right?

5 OBAN

PERTH 2

INVERNESS

4

ABERDEEN

3

GLASGOW

1

1.....................

2.....................

3.....................

4.....................

5.....................

ALL ALIKE?

These tractor pictures all look alike, but only two of them are the same. Which two?

A

B

C

D

E

F

G

H

CROSSWORD

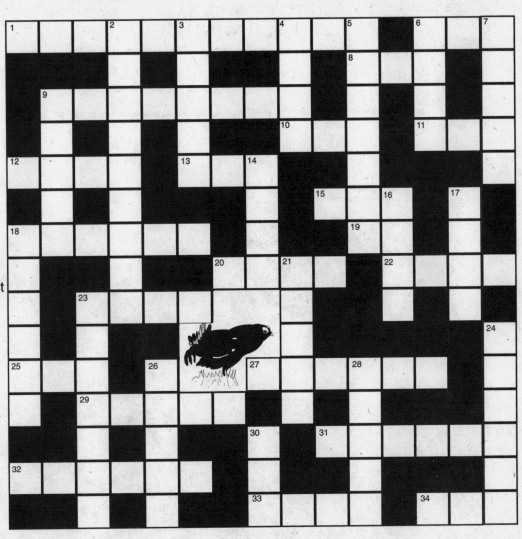

CLUES ACROSS

1. Famous Scottish poet (6,5)

6. and 7 down, Scotland's highest mountain (3,5)

8. Sweet or savoury pastry dish (3)

9. Hills of Skye (8)

10. You hear with this (3)

11. Used in a winter sport (3)

12. Hard-shelled sea creature (4)

13. A short sleep (3)

15. Scotland's longest river (3)

18. Famous Scottish outlaw (3,3)

19. Opposite of 'yes' (2)

20. Male deer (4)

22. Type of flower (4)

23. To melt (4)

25. Type of deer (3)

27. Pet name for Scottish monster (6)

29. A king or queen does this (5)

31. Scotland's largest loch (6)

32. Pictured bird (6)

33. See 26 down

34. Type of tree (3)

CLUES DOWN

2. Capital city of Scotland (9)

3. Eagle's claw (5)

4. "My Love Is Like A Red, Red ...."? (4)

5. Traditionally worn with the kilt (7)

6. Honey comes from these creatures (4)

7. See 6 across

9. A ship carries this (5)

14. Dug from bog for fuel (4)

16. Yellow part of an egg (4)

17. St Andrews is famous for this game (4)

18. '...... The Bruce' (6)

21. Scotland's only poisonous snake (5)

23. Another name for a vacuum flask (7)

24. 18 down met one of these in a cave (6)

26. and 33 across, Scots do this at New Year (5,4)

28. Famous monument in Princes Street, Edinburgh (5)

30. Small supernatural being (3)

ANSWERS

SPOT THE TWINS

These six Scottie dogs might all look the same, but only two are identical. Which two?

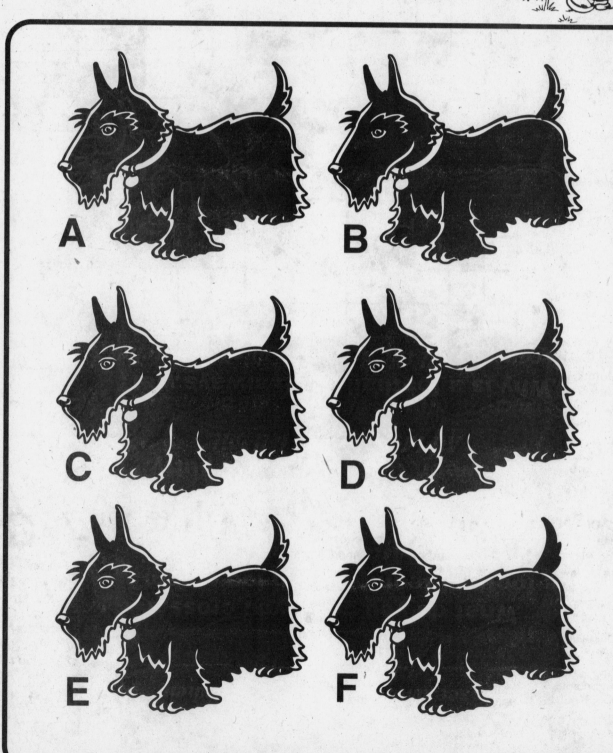

Why did Smiffy stand in front of the mirror with his eyes closed?
To see what he looked like when he was sleeping.

What do you get if you cross a football team with an ice cream?
Aston Vanilla!

Smiffy couldn't tell the difference between toothpaste and putty.
All his windows fell out.

Why is a football pitch always wet?
Because of all the dribbling during matches.

the Jocks and the Geordies

 ANGUS HECTOR SANDY WEE ECK BIG JOCK SIDNEY CEDRIC EGBERT ARNOLD LANKY

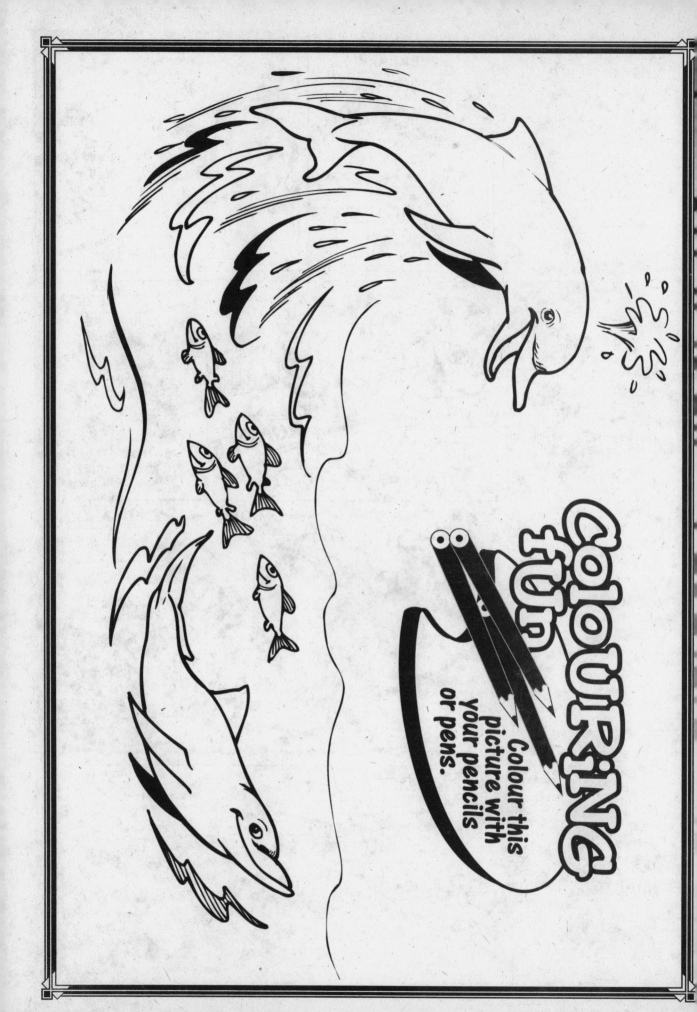

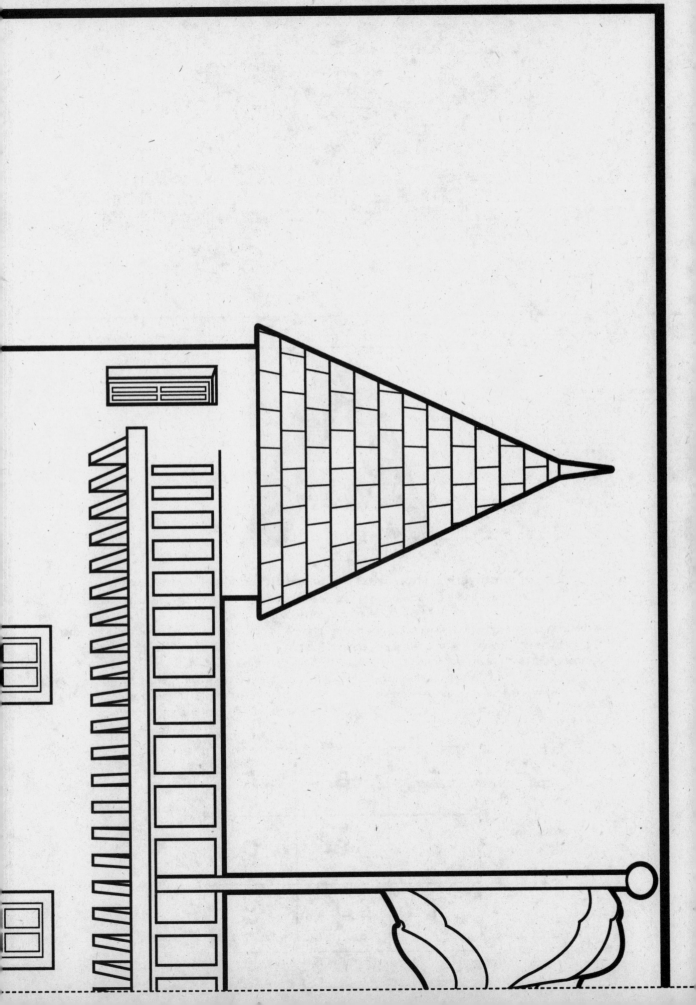

How to put together your Great Big Scottish Castle colouring poster.

Carefully tear out this page and the following eight poster pages. Then carefully finish trimming the pages by cutting along the dotted lines.

Paste the strip at the edge of the sheet B as shown, then place A in position to match the pictures together.

Do the same with sheets B and C. Now join sheets D, E and F and then G, H and I in the same way.

Next paste the strips of the attached sheets D, E and F. Stick down the sheets A, B and C to match the pictures together then do the same with sheets G, H and I. If you like you can make your poster stronger by turning it over and taping the edges together. Now you're ready to colour your poster.

Ask an adult to help you if you are not sure how to put this poster together.

C	B	A
F	E	D
I	H	G

BACK OF POSTER

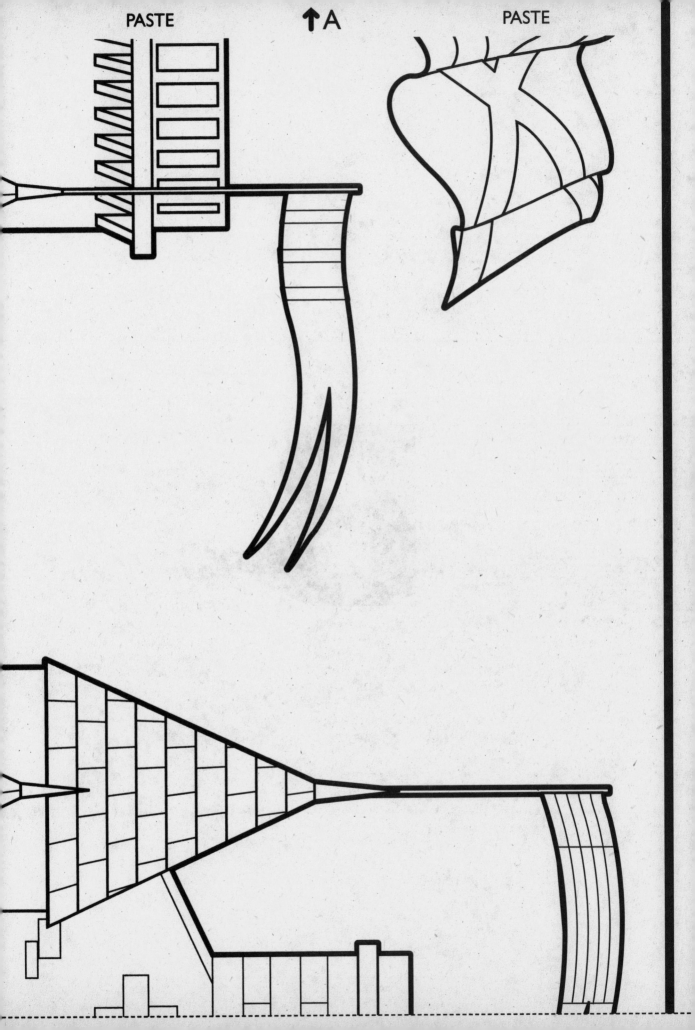

B

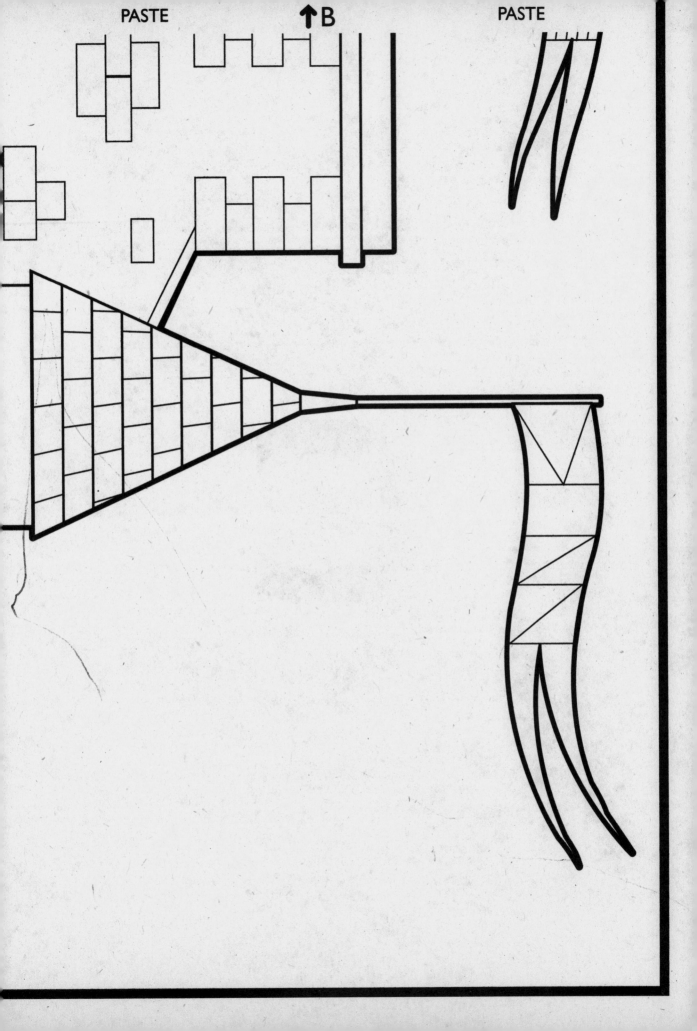

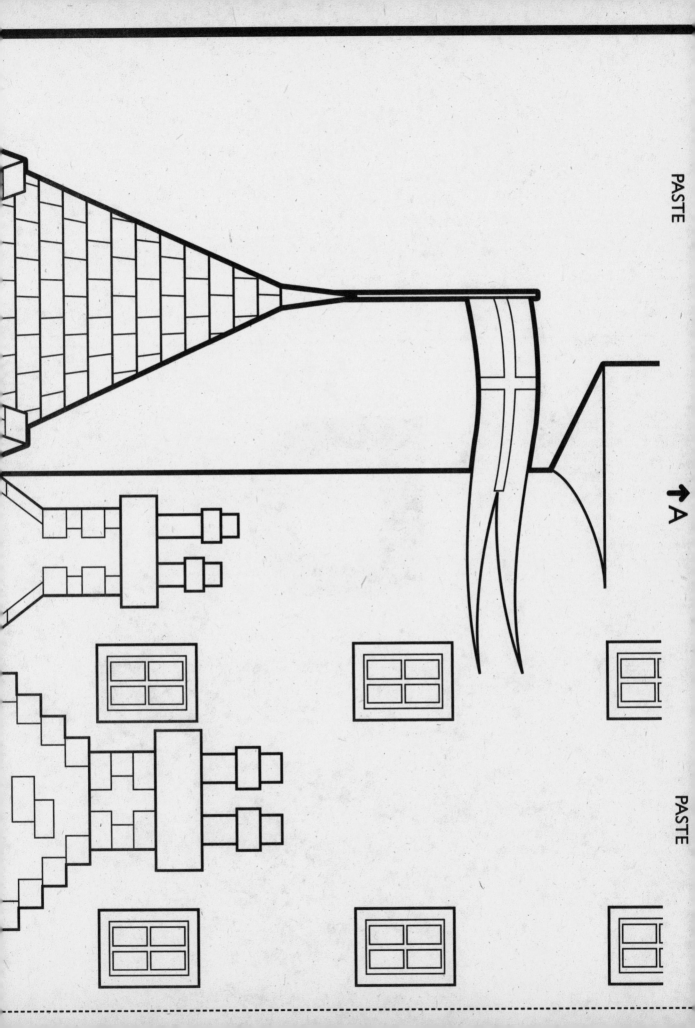

PASTE

PASTE

A

D

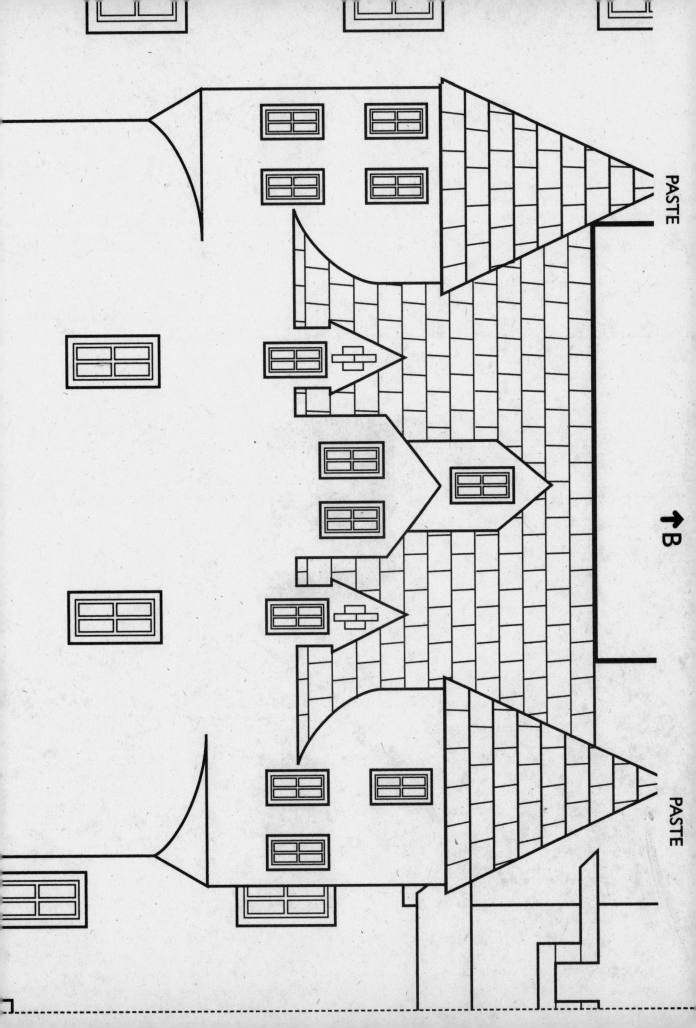

PASTE

→B

PASTE

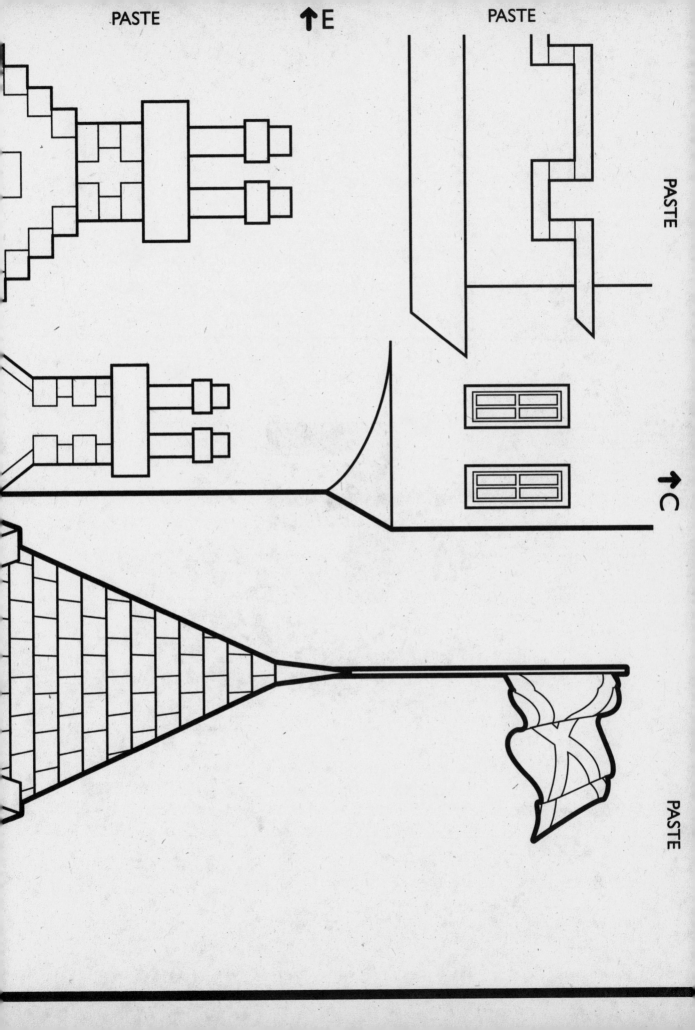

PASTE

↑E

PASTE

PASTE

↑C

PASTE

PASTE

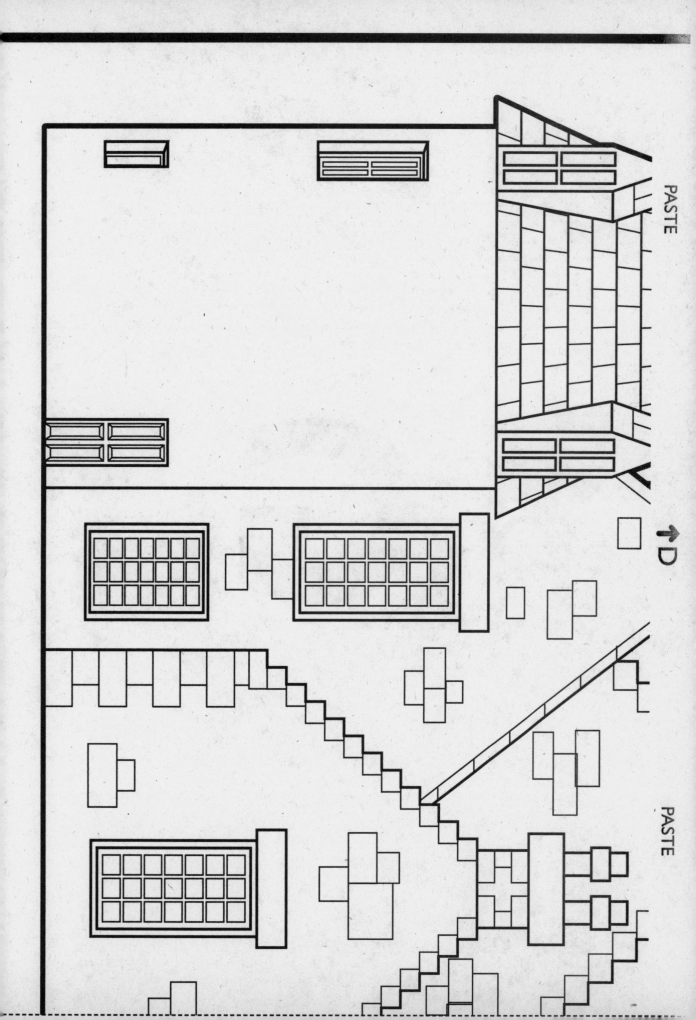

PASTE

PASTE

G

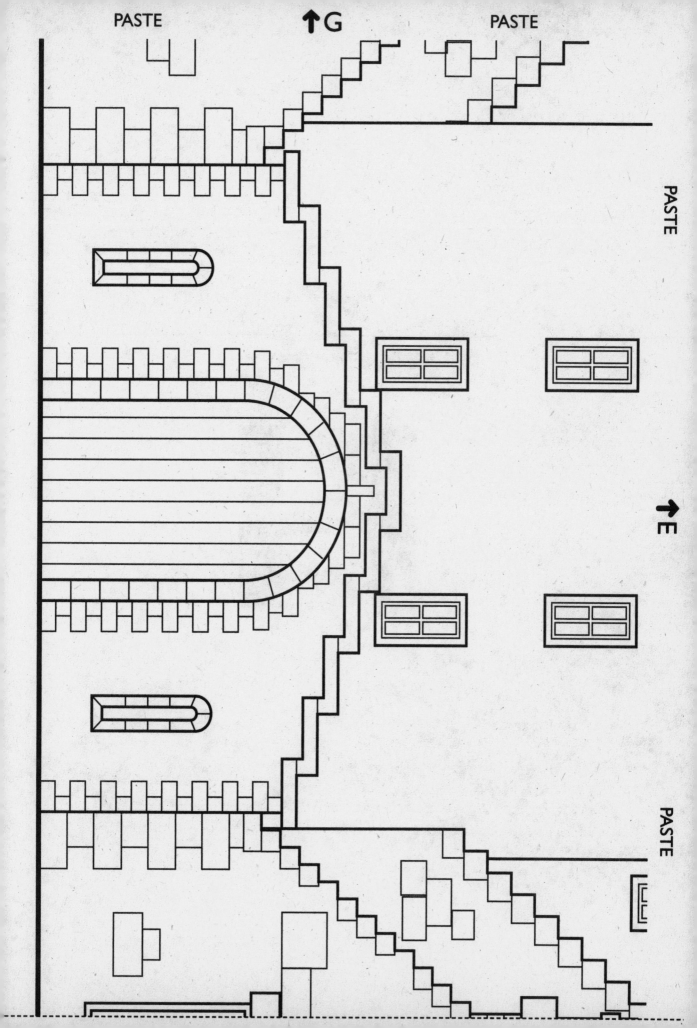

H

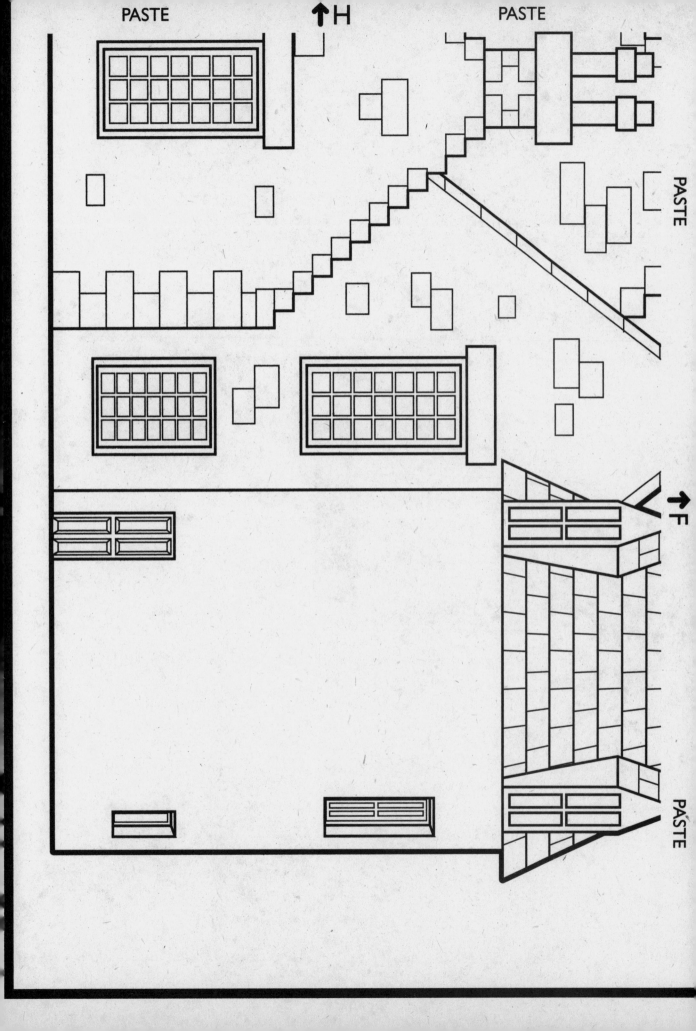

PASTE

PASTE

↑H

PASTE

→F

PASTE

BRIGHT IDEAS

SUN, SEA & SAND

Make pictures by using the sun. All you have to do is place a sheet of black paper in a sunny spot - a window sill is ideal. Cut out some simple shapes and place them on top of the paper. Leave the paper for a couple of weeks in the sun before removing the shapes to reveal your picture.

Building sandcastles is a fun thing to do at the beach, but there are other things you can make with sand too.

Try making sand sculptures of all sorts of things. Crocodiles, sharks and fish are just some of the creatures you can choose from. Add pieces of driftwood, shells and seaweed to make them look more interesting.

Drawing pictures in the sand is lots of fun, especially if your friends or family join in. You can make your pictures huge with all sorts of detail.

If you are out for a walk on the beach, see how many types of footprints you can find in the sand. See how they differ in size and depth depending on the size and weight of the creatures that made them.

Searching in rock pools can be fun. There are often all sorts of sea creatures to be found there – crabs, small fish hiding in seaweed and sea anenomes and limpets clinging to the rocks. You can sometimes find several varieties of seaweed there, too.

Count how many different types of creatures you can see, but never remove them from the safety of the pool and never try to prise clinging animals from the rocks.

Always ask an adult to go with you when you are close to deep water.

The Jocks and the Geordies

 ANGUS
 HECTOR
 SANDY
 WEE ECK
 BIG JOCK
 SIDNEY
 CEDRIC
 EBBERT
 ARNOLD
 LANKY

BRR! IT'S FREEZIN' AND WE'RE REALLY HARD UP!

SHIVER!

SO HARD UP, SIDNEY'S EATING A STRONG MINT AND WE'RE SITTING AROUND HIM TO KEEP WARM!

MINTY GLOW

CHATTER!

LET'S BELT THE JOCKS — THAT'LL WARM OUR HANDS UP!

GOOD IDEA!

JOCK HUT

HEY! LET'S HAVE SOME OF YOUR SPARE COAL!

OOFYAH!

WHUMP!

WALLOP!

BASH!

CERTAINLY! HERE YOU ARE!

JOCK HUT

YOU KNOW US — WE'RE ALL HEART!

LET'S GIVE THE JOCKS THIS!

POPPING CORN

HUH? AFTER WHAT THEY'VE DONE, YOU WANT TO GIVE THEM A PRESENT?

I'M JUST THE FORGIVING TYPE!

HOO! HE'S POURING IT DOWN THE JOCKS' CHIMNEY!

And—

BDOING! KERPOP! BDANG!

JOCK HUT

ERK! SOMEBODY'S CHUCKED A BUCKET O' BULLETS DOWN OUR CHIMNEY!

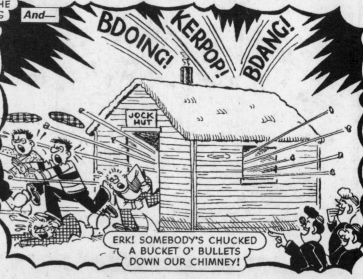

Word Square

How many times does the word "tablet" appear in the word square?

T	A	B	L	E	T
A	A	L	A	E	A
B	L	B	L	T	B
L	A	B	L	B	L
E	A	T	B	E	E
T	A	B	L	E	T

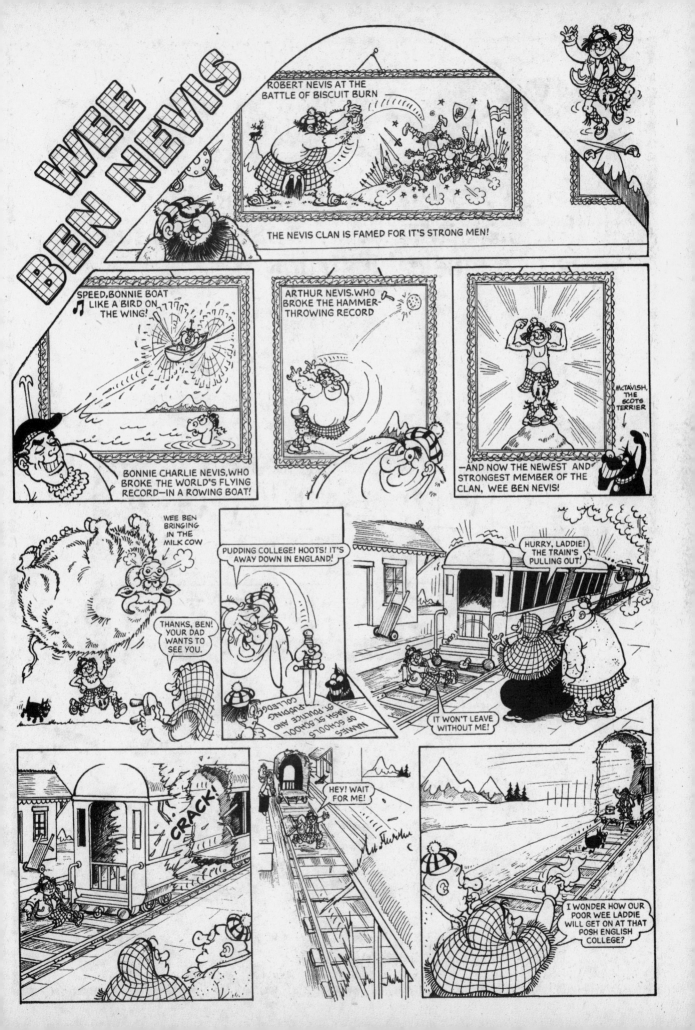

WORD Puzzle

Can you complete the words reading down so that the centre row across spells the name of a musical instrument?

E	C	A	S	T	A	G	A
B	T	O	Y	N	T	T	H

HAGGIS ATTACK!

You're camping in the Highlands and your tent is surrounded by long-eared, hairy-kneed haggis. Draw what you think they would look like.

Draw suitable pictures for the front of these holiday postcards.

Dunvegan Castle – Skye

The River Forth Railway Bridge

the Jocks and the Geordies

ANGUS · HECTOR · SANDY · WEE ECK · BIG JOCK · SIDNEY · CEDRIC · EGBERT · ARNOLD · LANKY

COLOURING FUN

Use your pencils or pens to colour this Scottish flag.

FLYING HIGH

Can you spot which bird silhouette is the odd one out?

A

B

C

D

E

LIMERICK FUN

A farmer from near the
Queen's View
Bought a beautiful, red,
Highland coo.
He bathed her to go,
To the Pitlochry show,
And used all his wife's best
shampoo.

There was a young girl
from Dunoon,
Who wanted to fly to the moon.
She built a small rocket,
That fitted her pocket,
And she should be
arriving quite soon.

A downhearted Scotsman felt
grave,
As he hid all alone in a cave.
He found inspiration
And saved his great nation.
From a spider came 'Scotland
the Brave'!

Scottish Tourist QUIZ

1. Where in Angus is the Reekie Linn waterfall? Is it Glen Clova, Glenisla or Glen Prosen?
2. What is Skara Brae?
3. Where is Skara Brae?
4. Where would you go to see the Stone of Destiny?
5. In which river will you see the Bass Rock?
6. Which Scottish attraction became a World Heritage Site in 2001?
7. Where is the Royal Mile?
8. In which Scottish City can you visit Discovery Point?
9. Which monument sits on the Abbey Craig near Stirling?
10. On which island are the Callanish Standing Stones situated - Iona, Mull or Lewis?
11. Abbotsford, near Melrose was the home of which Scottish writer? Was it Sir Arthur Conan Doyle, Robert Louis Stevenson or Sir Walter Scott?
12. What stretches 95 miles from Milngavie to Fort William?
13. Which part of the coastal area of Scotland is known as the East Neuk?
14. Which famous landmark overlooks Loch Tummel?
15. Urquhart Castle can be found beside which Scottish loch?

ANSWERS: 1. Glenisla; 2. A stone-age village; 3. Orkney; 4. Edinburgh Castle; 5. The River Forth; 6. New Lanark; 7. Edinburgh; 8. Dundee; 9. The Wallace Monument; 10. Lewis; 11. Sir Walter Scott; 12. The West Highland Way; 13. Fife; 14. The Queen's View; 15. Loch Ness.

Which of these pictures below is the odd one out?

IN THE CLOUDS

A

B

C

D

E

F

Get Shirty

Draw a design and slogan for a Scottish T-shirt.

Thistle Be Fun!

By using only the letters in

THISTLE

can you find five four-letter words to fit the following descriptions?

1. Thin opening. ....

2. Sediment. ....

3. Binds. ....

4. Place. ....

5. Put in order. ....

The Jocks and the Geordies

HIDDEN THISTLES

There are six small thistles hidden in this page. How quickly can you find them?

Doctor, doctor. Every time I drink a cup of hot tea, I get a pain in my eye.
Try taking the spoon out.

Why is it useless telling shopkeepers to be quiet?
Because they don't shut up till the end of the day.

THE 'A' TEAMS

Name five
Scottish
football teams
starting with
the letter 'A'.

Arbroath, Ayr, Alloa,
Aberdeen, Albion.

ANSWER

HOCKEY PUZZLER

Only two of those silhouettes are the same. Can you find them?

A

B

C

D

E

F

G

H

I

ANSWER: B F

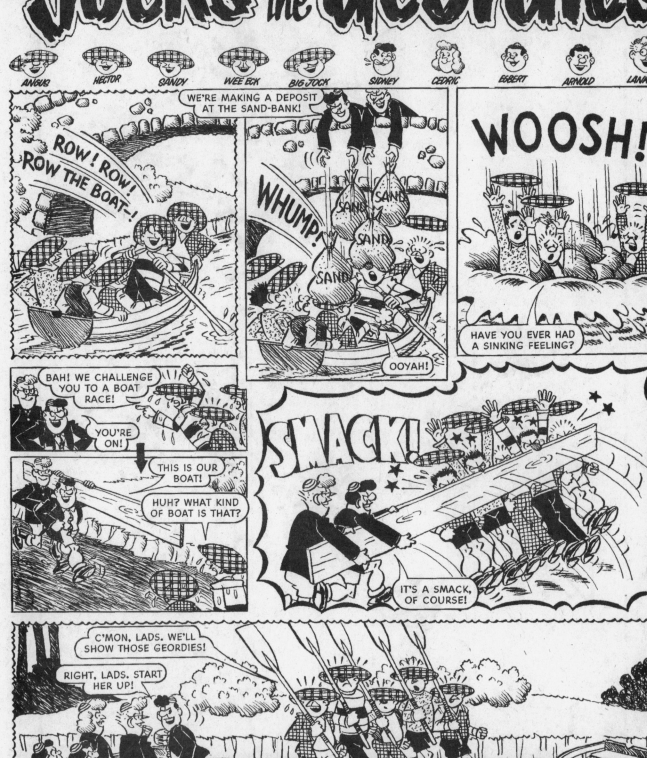

Take A Letter

Take the initial letters of the following objects and rearrange them into a famous Scottish celebration

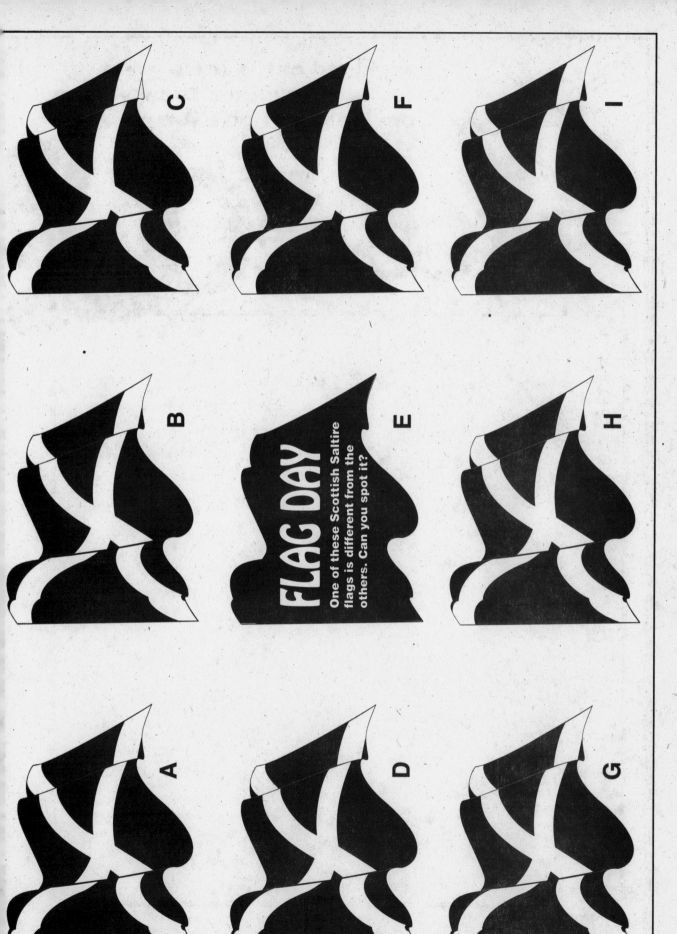

FLAG DAY

One of these Scottish Saltire flags is different from the others. Can you spot it?

Highland cattle are a great tourist attraction. Draw your own one here and give it a name.

MOO-OCO!

SCOTTISH WORD SEARCH

All the Scottish places in this wordsearch begin with the letter 'S'.
How many can you find? The letters can be read up, down, backwards or diagonally.

The letters in the black squares will spell the name of a Scottish mountain.

STRATHKINNESS
STRATHCARRON
SPITTAL
STROMNESS
SKYE
STIRLING
STROMEFERRY
SALTCOATS
SKIRZA
SUNART
SANDAY
STRATHMORE
STRANRAER
SCAPA FLOW
SANQUAR
STORNOWAY
SEIL
SOAY
SALINE
SALEN
SORN
SCOURIE
SHIEL (GLEN)
SCONE
SCARP

S	S	E	N	M	O	R	T	S	V	R	S	R
T	T	C	E	I	R	U	O	C	S	E	U	P
R	I	R	S	T	O	R	N	O	W	A	Y	N
A	R	S	A	H	N	S	I	S	Z	R	W	E
T	L	A	T	T	I	P	S	R	S	N	O	R
H	I	L	E	I	H	S	I	A	C	A	L	O
C	N	E	Y	E	Y	K	S	U	O	R	F	M
A	G	N	A	E	S	H	I	Q	N	T	A	H
R	S	I	D	U	A	L	L	N	E	S	P	T
R	C	L	N	L	I	S	I	A	N	O	A	A
O	A	A	A	E	Y	A	O	S	N	E	C	R
N	R	S	S	T	A	O	C	T	L	A	S	T
T	P	Y	R	R	E	F	E	M	O	R	T	S

The hidden Scottish mountain is Schiehallion.

NAME THE CITY

See if you can help –
Rearrange the initial letter of the objects shown to
spell the name of a Scottish city.

_ _ _ _ _

MUXED IP!

These Scottish city names have got all mixed up. Can you sort them?

Abergow Dunness Glasdee Inverburgh Edindeen

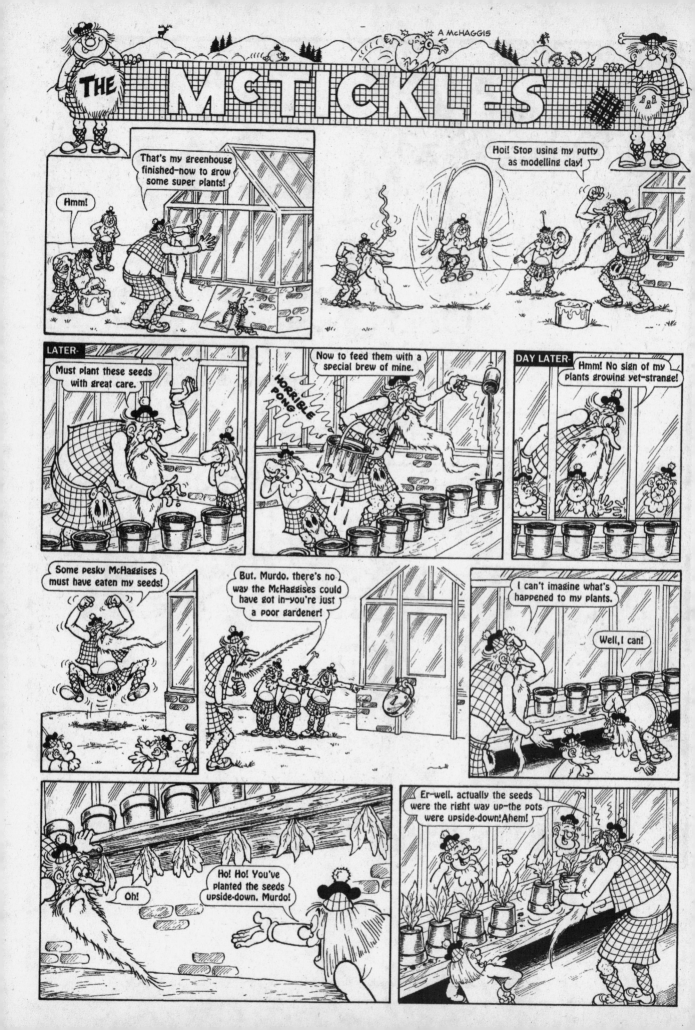

MISSING TOWNS

The Scottish places listed below all start with a vowel (A E I O U). Can you complete the names?

__ BERDEEN

__ RBROATH

__ AST KILBRIDE

__ NVERNESS

__ RVINE

__ BAN

__ LLAPOOL

MISSING!

A

B

C

D

Look carefully at this piece of tartan Now look at the pictures above. Which one is the missing piece?

RAINY DAYS

Only two of these pictures are exactly the same. Can you find them?

A

B

C

D

E

F

G

H

I

marathon mix-up

Hamish is running in the marathon. Can you unscramble the following groups of letters to find five words which mean 'fast'?

YDEESP   **UKQIC**

WSFTI   **EFLET**

RPDIA

START

ZIP

The Jocks and the Geordies

ANGUS HECTOR SANDY WEE ECK BIG JOCK SIDNEY CEDRIC EGBERT ARNOLD LANKY

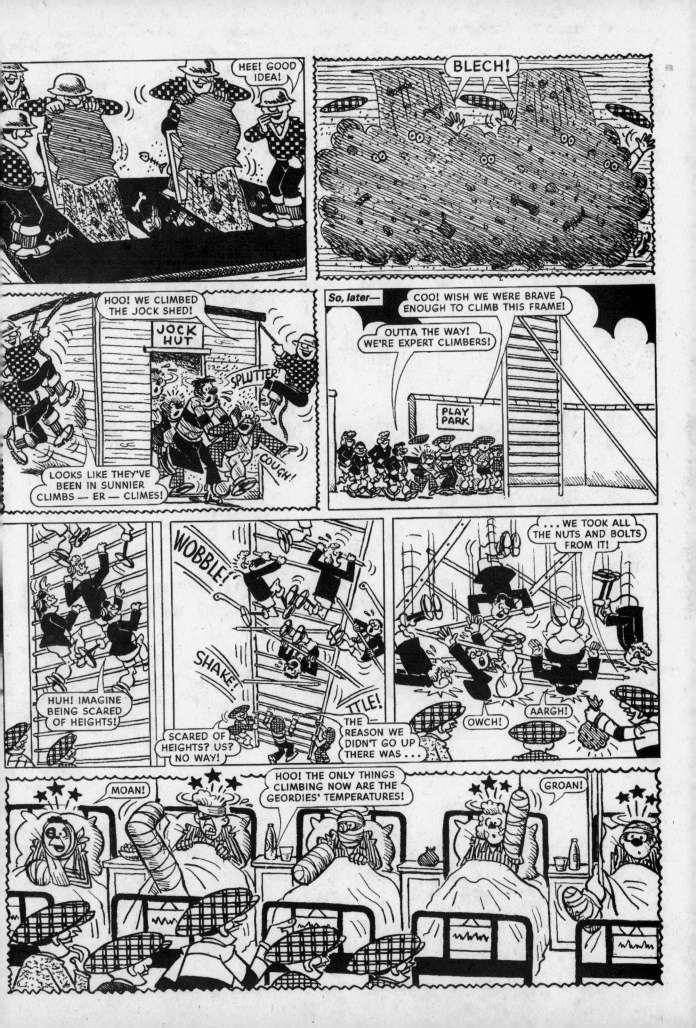

Know Your Animals

1. What is a Scottish Blackface?

2. What is a Gordon Setter?

3. What is a Belted Galloway?

4. What is a Scottish Fold?

5. What is a Scottish Cashmere?

6. What is a Clydesdale?

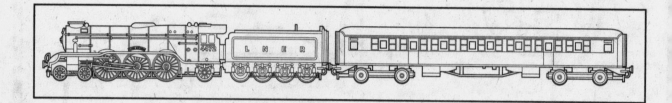

How to put together your train colouring frieze.

Carefully tear out this page and the following five poster pages. Then carefully finish trimming the pages by cutting along the dotted lines.

Paste the strip at the edge of the sheet B as shown, then place A in position to match the pictures together. Do the same with Sheets, B, C, D, E and F.

If you like you can make your poster stronger by turning it over and taping the edges together. Now you're ready to colour your frieze.

Ask an adult to help you if you are not sure how to put this frieze together.

F	E	D	C	B	A

BACK OF POSTER

PASTE ↑A PASTE

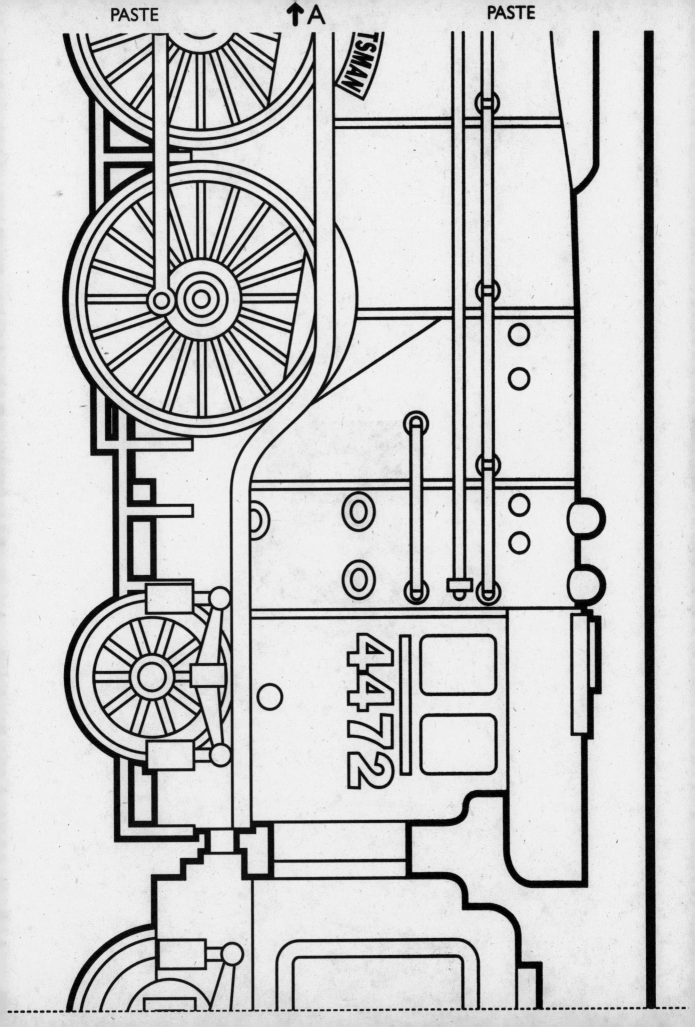

B

↑B

L

N

E

R

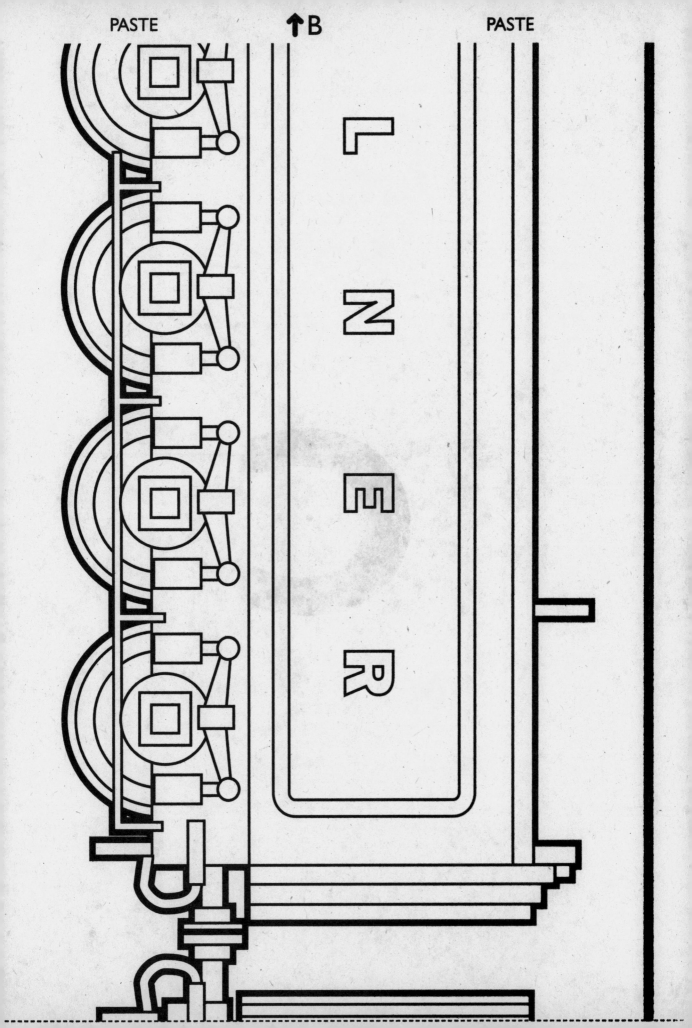

PASTE

↑C

PASTE

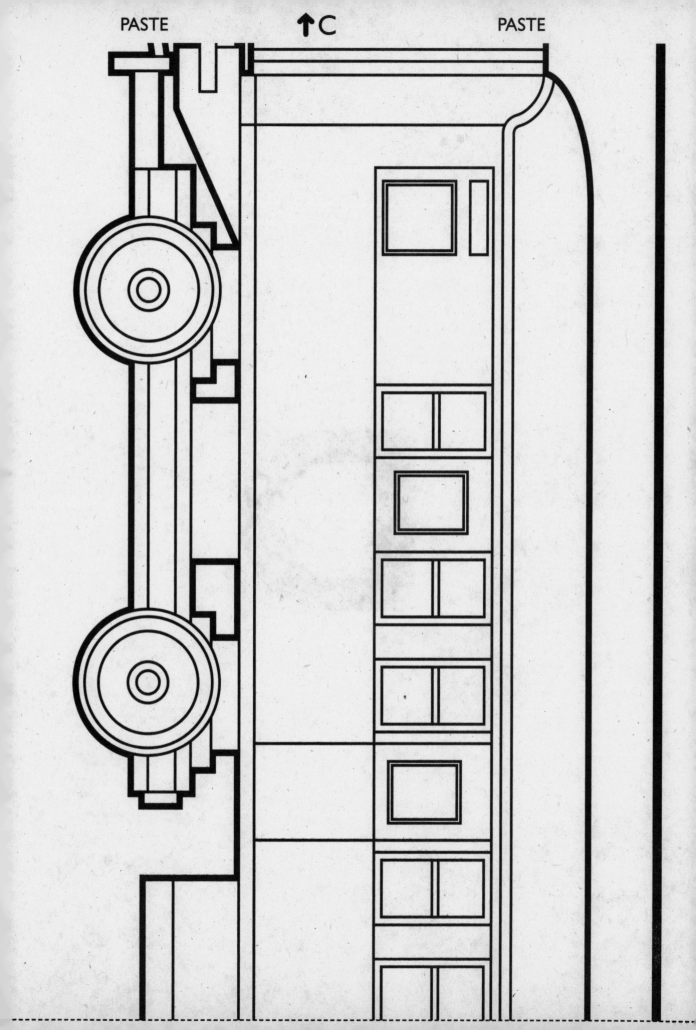

PASTE

↑C

PASTE

D

PASTE

↑D

PASTE

PASTE

PASTE

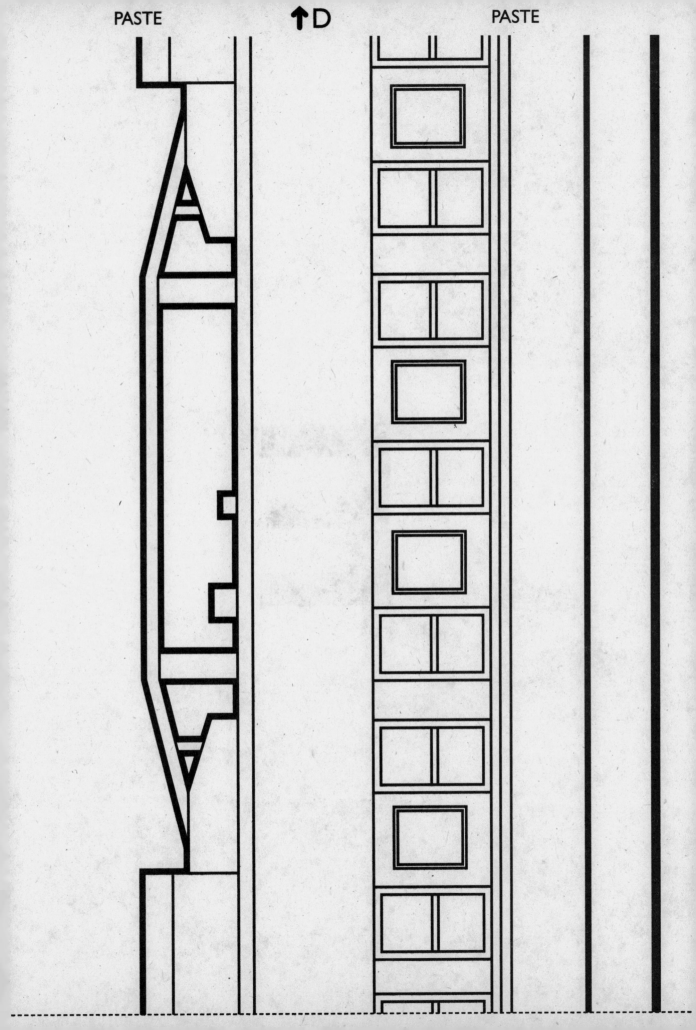

PASTE

↑E

PASTE

PASTE

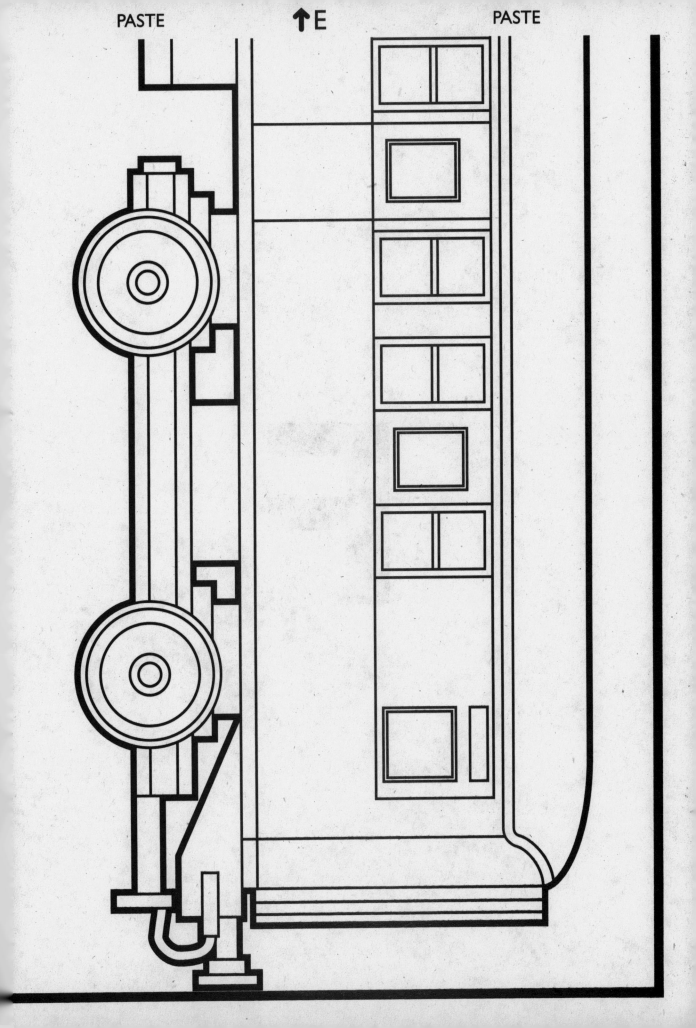

LIMERICK FUN

A hairy wee dug frae Stranraer,
Loved travelling around in the car!
He'd jump on to the seat,
Wouldn't lie at your feet,
And sleep all the way
to Dunbar.

A gardener from north
of Dundee
Starting digging to
plant a new tree.
For ten hours or more
He dug through the
earth's core,
And landed in Melbourne
for tea.

A keen lady curler from Dyce
Slipped while taking her
turn on the ice.
She shot down the rink,
Then said with a wink,
"Stick to bowling greens, that's
my advice!"

the Jocks and the Geordies

HIDDEN **haggis**

How many times can you find the word **HAGGIS** hidden in the word square?

A	H	S	I	G	G	A	H	H	A	H
I	S	H	H	H	I	A	A	A	H	A
S	I	I	A	A	G	H	G	G	A	G
I	G	A	G	G	A	A	G	G	G	G
G	G	I	G	G	S	I	I	I	G	I
G	A	S	S	I	A	I	S	S	I	S
A	H	A	G	S	A	H	S	H	S	I
H	A	G	G	I	S	A	A	S	H	G
G	G	A	H	A	G	G	I	S	A	G
H	A	G	G	I	S	G	A	I	G	A
H	A	G	G	I	S	I	G	G	A	H

Jumbled Islands

Unscramble the groups of letters to find the names of five Scottish islands

ESKY

WELIS

MURH

CKUM

GGIE

IN FLIGHT

Two of these pictures are different from the others. Can you spot them?

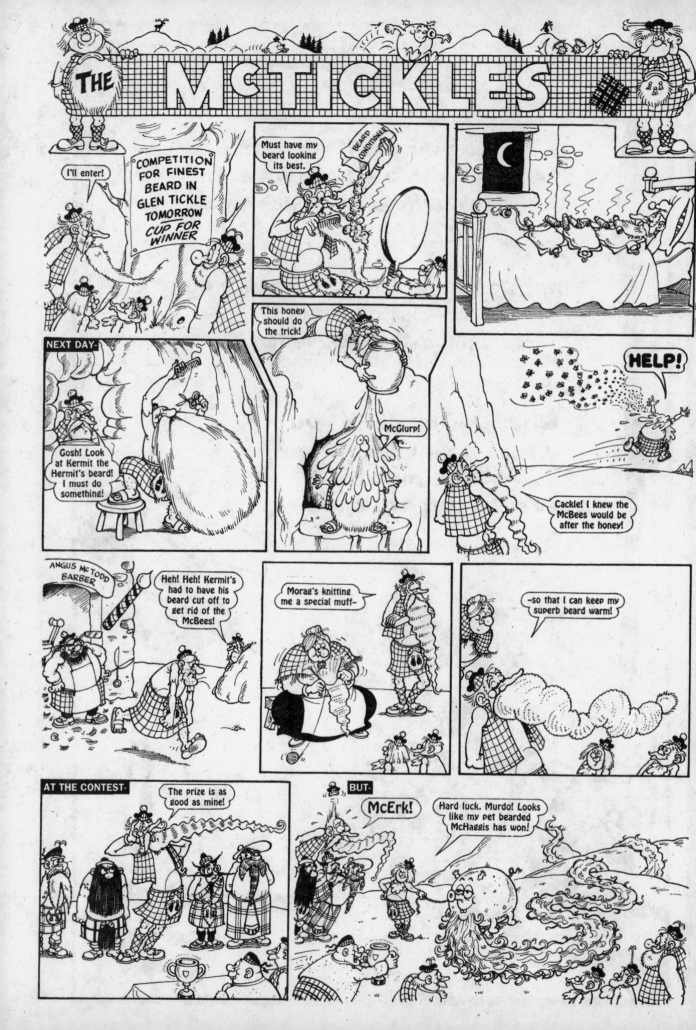

MY VERY OWN TARTAN

Design your own tartan in the frame and letter your name in the box below.

JIGSAW PUZZLER

To complete the jigsaw puzzle can you choose the correct piece from the ones shown below?

 **A**

B

 **C**

ANSWER: B

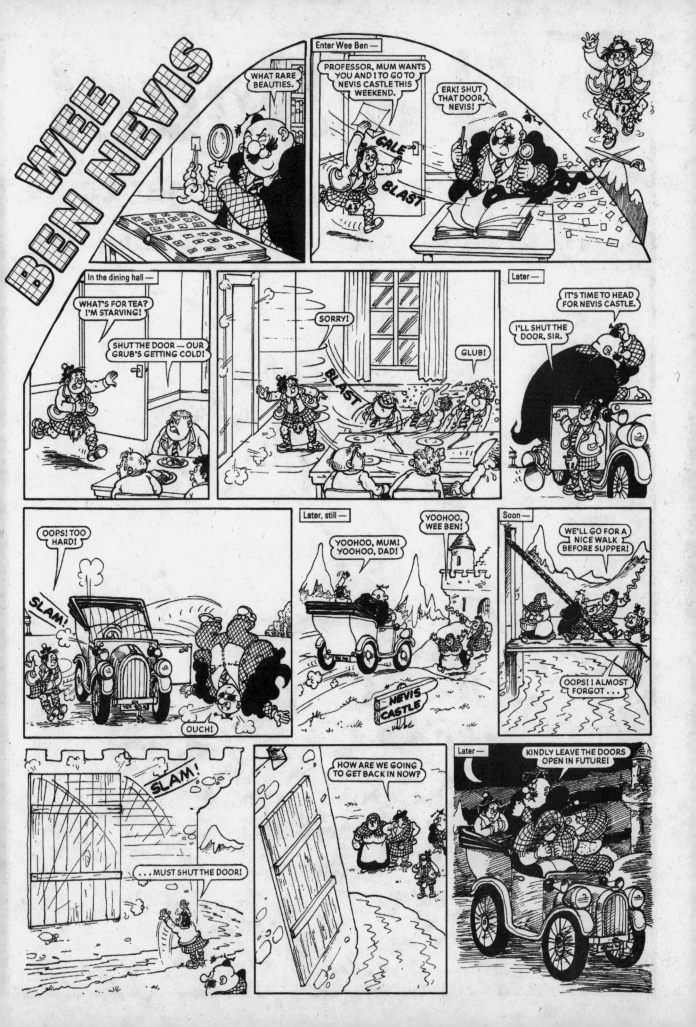

In the Soup!

Rearrange the pasta shapes to give you a type of soup.

ABC PASTA

OH C R
B S H T
C T O

ANSWER: SCOTCH BROTH

ON COURSE

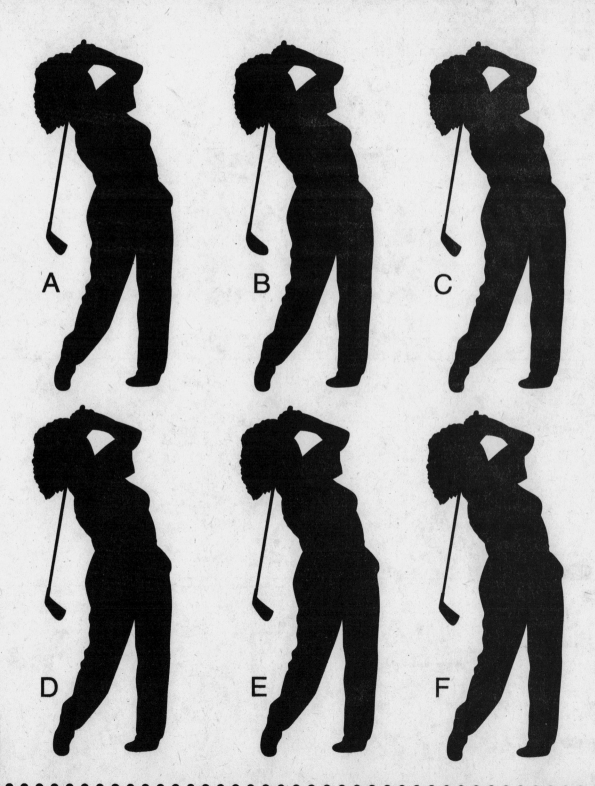

A

B

C

D

E

F

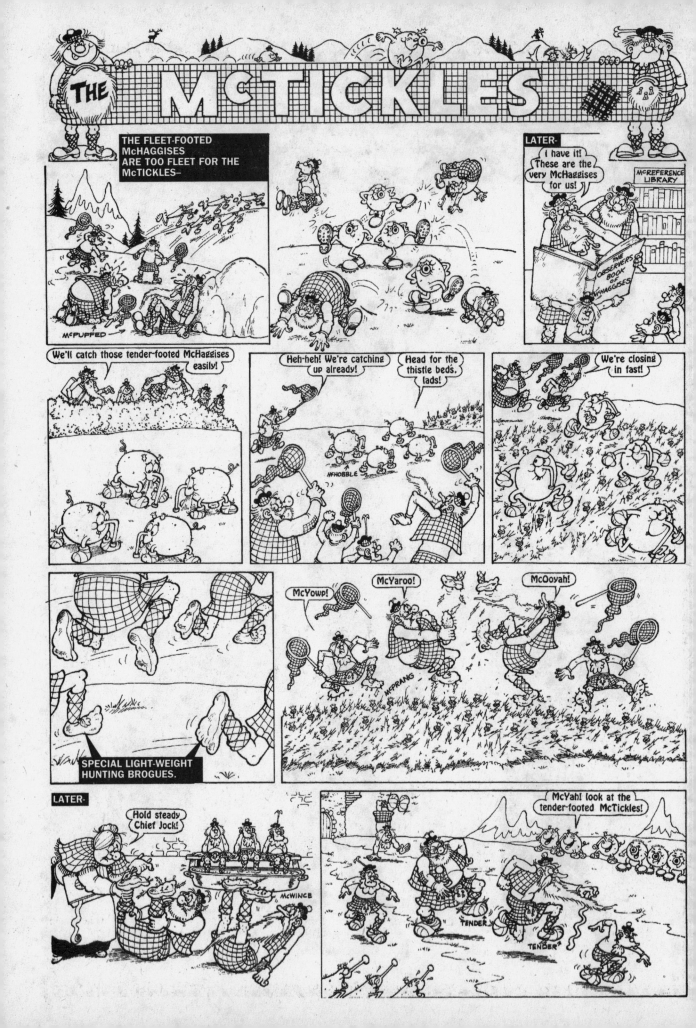

HOW MANY?

How many words of three letters can you make from the word

SCOTLAND?

HOOCH!

Complete the names of these Scottish dances.

1. **The Sailor's**
   - - - - - - - -

2. **The Highland**
   - - - - -

3. **The Sword**
   - - - - -

GREAT SCOT!

The following boys' names can be found in the wordsearch. How quickly can you find them all?

R	O	D	E	R	I	C	K	P	X	J	A
A	G	O	R	D	O	N	E	M	W	D	L
N	I	N	I	A	N	I	N	N	E	S	A
D	L	A	C	H	L	A	N	E	I	L	S
R	P	L	Y	W	V	I	E	A	M	B	D
E	T	D	C	Q	N	N	T	N	A	G	A
W	R	H	A	M	I	S	H	G	J	I	I
E	A	E	L	F	E	R	G	U	S	A	R
C	W	P	U	U	F	R	A	S	E	R	O
U	E	J	M	A	L	C	O	L	M	C	R
R	T	A	E	Z	N	T	S	A	N	D	Y
B	S	C	A	M	E	R	O	N	B	R	Q

ALASDAIR   EUAN   NEIL   LACHLAN
BRUCE   FERGUS   STEWART   RODERICK
CRAIG   JAMIE   FRASER   DONALD
RORY   CALUM   KENNETH   GORDON
ANGUS   SEUMAS   HAMISH   MALCOLM
CAMERON   IAIN   ANDREW
SANDY   INNES   NINIAN

the Jocks and the Geordies

 ANGUS
 HECTOR
 SANDY
 WEE ECK
 BIG JOCK
 SIDNEY
 CEDRIC
 EBBERT
 ARNOLD
 LANKY

FOOTBALL CRAZY!

Jumbled up on the footballs
are the names of six Scottish
football teams.
How quickly can you unscramble
them all?

LOok Carefully

Look carefully at these thistle pictures and try to spot the odd-one-out.

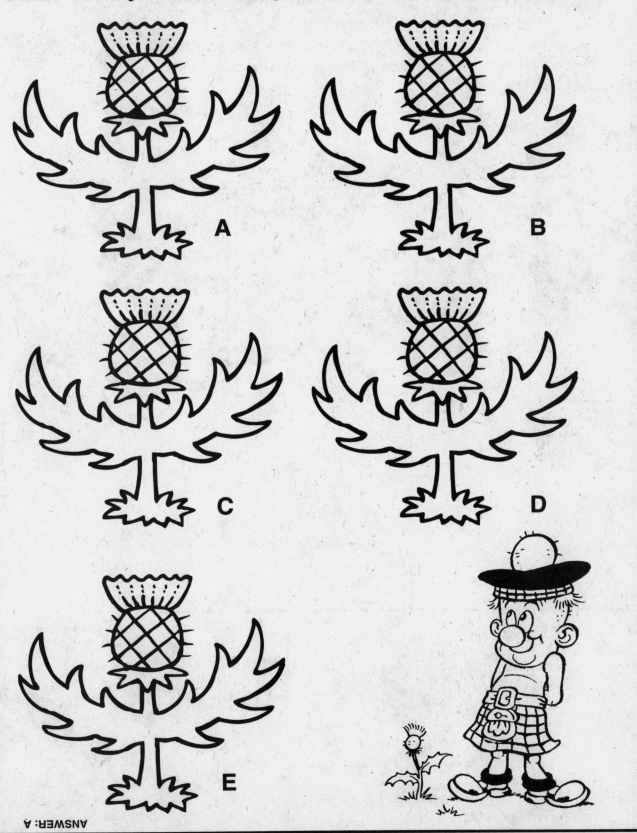

A

B

C

D

E

FOOD SCRAMBLE

Unscramble the mixed-up words to find some traditional Scottish food and place in the squares below. When you have unscrambled the letters, you will find that the letters in the shaded squares will reveal another Scottish favourite.

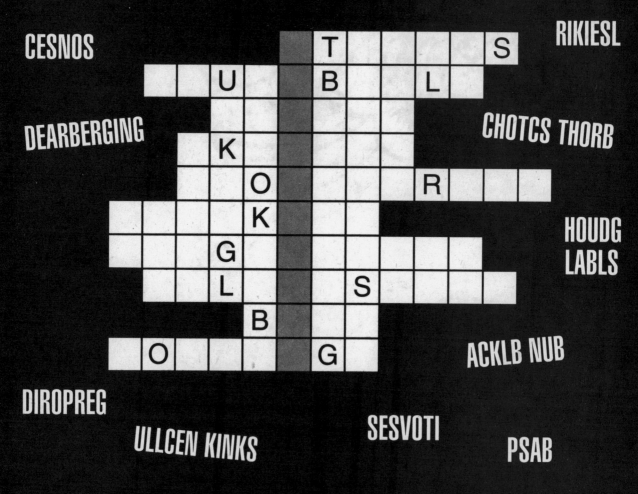

CESNOS

RIKIESL

DEARBERGING

CHOTCS THORB

HOUDG LABLS

ACKLB NUB

DIROPREG

ULLCEN KINKS

SESVOTI

PSAB

FOOD FOR THOUGHT

Once you've solved the following clues, the initial letters of each object, when rearranged will give you something which Scots people like to eat!

1. A game in which you can score an eagle
2. Animals with incredibly long necks
3. Red Rum was a famous one
4. Name of the Queen's daughter
5. Rome is the capital city of this country
6. Edinburgh is its capital city

WORD
PUZZLE

How many words of three letters can you make from the letters in

SALTIRE

PEDAL POWER

Two of these cyclists are exactly the same. Can you spot them?

What do you call a cow eating grass in your front garden?
A lawn mooer!

What do you call a person who rolls in the mud then crosses the road twice?
A dirty double crosser.

Why did six planks stand in a circle?
They were having a board meeting.

Why is a red headed idiot like a biscuit?
He's a ginger nut!

What's an alien's favourite sweet?
Martian Mallows.

MONSTER FUN

Draw what you think the Loch Ness Monster looks like.

Do You Know?

1. In a Scottish surname, what does the 'Mac' stand for?

2. What is cullen skink? Is it a) an animal b) a soup c) a cloud formation?

3. In which Scottish city would you find The Mound?

4. In which town was Ewan MacGregor brought up?

5. What is the national emblem of Scotland?

6. Which Scottish town is known as 'the home of golf'?

7. In which city would you find Buchanan Street Station?

8. What are The Outer Hebrides?

9. If the weather is dreich, is that good or bad?

10. What are the main ingredients of tablet?

ANSWERS: 1. Son of, 2. It's a soup, 3. Edinburgh, 4. Crieff, 5. Thistle, 6. St Andrews, 7. Glasgow, 8. A group of islands, 9. Very bad! 10. Sugar, condensed milk and butter.

BE SMART!

By using only the letters in 'Highland' can you find five four-letter words to fit the following definitions–

1. Part of the body

2. Type of weather

3. Happy

4. Clock face

5. Put down flat

BACKWARD NOTICE

Can you read this notice without looking in a mirror?

What A Discovery

One of these silhouettes of the SS Discovery is different from the others. Can you spot it?

A

B

C

D

Which footballers wear matches in their hair?
Strikers!

What do snake charmers feed their snakes on?
Self-raising flour!

Angler – You've been watching me for three hours. Why don't you try fishing yourself?
Smiffy – No, I don't have the patience.

Actor – Did Jones get his new play used?
Producer – Yes, the stage manager tore up the manuscript and used it in a snow-storm scene.

Simon – Did you hear the joke about the rope?
May – No.
Simon – Oh, skip it!

What did the north wind say to the south wind?
Let's play draughts.

What's a pig's favourite football team?
Queen's Pork Rangers.

Jill – Did you hear about the man who said he was listening to the match?
Jack – No, tell me.
Jill – He burned his ear!

Mum – You can't come in the house unless your feet are clean!
Minnie – They are clean, Mum. It's only my shoes that are dirty!

What did Dracula say when the dentist wanted to pull out his teeth?
No fangs!

BARMY BOOKS
The Unwelcome Visitor by Gladys Gone.
Gone Shopping by Carrie R. Bag.
Who's to Blame? by E.Z.E. Diddit.
The Invitation by Willie B. Cumming.

What did the bald man say when he got a comb?
I'll never part with you!

Knock! Knock!
Who's there?
A little old lady.
A little old lady who?
I didn't know you could yodel!

What did the orange squash say to the water?
I'm diluted to meet you!

Smith – Why are you talking to yourself?
Jones – First, because I want to talk to a sensible man and second, because I like to hear a sensible man talking to me.

Tom – I'm thinking of going to America. What will it cost me?
Travel agent – Nothing.
Tom – What do you mean?
Travel agent – Well, it doesn't cost anything to think.

Boxer – You're a poor publicity man. I win a fight and all you get me in the paper is four columns.
Publicity agent – What are you grumbling for? Look at the big fights Nelson won and he only got one column.

Interviewer – Are you quick?
Job applicant – Quick? Why, I blew out the candle last night and was in bed and asleep before the room was dark.

Minnie – I want to ask you a question, Mum.
Mother – Well, go ahead.
Minnie – When a hole appears in a pair of tights, what becomes of the piece of material that was there before the hole appeared?

Tim – Don't be afraid of my dog. If he thinks you're afraid, he'll bite off your hand.
Tom – That's what I'm afraid of.

Draw suitable pictures for the front of these holiday postcards.

McCaig's Folly – Oban

Brodick Castle – Isle of Arran

Animal Puzzler

Unscramble the letters below to find the names of 10 animals. When you have unscrambled them put the names of the animals that can be found in the wild in Scotland into the puzzle boxes to reveal another Scottish animal hidden in the shaded squares.

BITABR **VEBEAR** **RETTO** **FLOW** **ERD** **ERED** **OHGHEGDE**

ASTOA **XYNL** **RIQULERS** **AREB**

SMART ART!

Fill in the outline to see how closely you can copy the picture of the piper.

A-MAZE-ING!

Help the little Scottie find its way through the maze to it's bone.

The Jocks and the Geordies

 ANGUS HECTOR SANDY WEE ECK BIG JOCK SIDNEY CEDRIC EGBERT ARNOLD LANKY

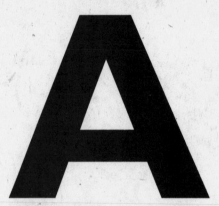

How to put together your Loch Ness Monster colouring poster.

Carefully tear out this page and the following three poster pages. Then carefully finish trimming the pages by cutting along the dotted lines.

Paste the strip at the foot of the sheet A as shown, then place B in position to match the pictures together. Do the same with sheets C and D.

Next paste the strips of the attached sheets C and D. Stick down the sheets A and B to make the picture complete. If you like you can make your poster stronger by turning it over and taping the edges together. Now you're ready to colour your poster.

Ask an adult to help you if you are not sure how to put this poster together.

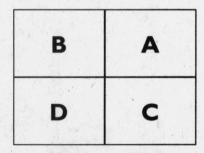

BACK OF POSTER

B

D

Hidden Scotland

How many times can you find the word SCOTLAND hidden in the square?

S	N	D	L	O	S	S	S	D	D	S
C	S	A	N	T	C	C	N	D	N	C
O	D	C	C	A	O	A	N	S	A	D
T	S	T	O	T	L	A	D	D	L	N
L	C	O	L	T	L	T	N	O	T	A
A	N	A	O	T	L	A	O	T	O	L
N	N	C	O	A	L	A	L	C	C	T
D	S	C	O	T	L	A	N	D	S	O
L	S	C	O	T	L	A	N	D	O	C
A	D	C	D	N	A	L	T	O	C	S
N	S	C	O	T	L	A	N	D	S	C

LIMERICK FUN

There was a young boy from the West,
Who was a terrible pest.
His mum got real mad
And so did his dad
When he fished with his grandad's string vest!

A footballing fan from Prestwick,
Ate too many pies for a trick.
He got on the bus,
Made a terrible fuss
Then had to get off to be sick!

There was a young girl from Montrose,
Who had a terrible cold in her nose.
She felt quite unwell
And of course, couldn't smell
Hence the terrible perfume she chose!

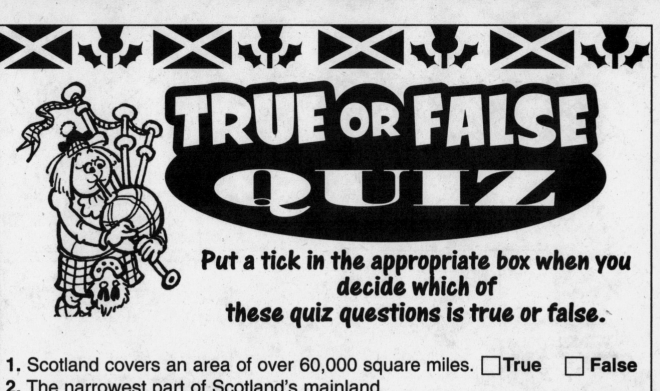

TRUE OR FALSE QUIZ

Put a tick in the appropriate box when you decide which of these quiz questions is true or false.

1. Scotland covers an area of over 60,000 square miles. ☐ True ☐ False
2. The narrowest part of Scotland's mainland measures just 25 miles. ☐ True ☐ False
3. There are over 787 islands in Scotland. ☐ True ☐ False
4. Scotland's furthest point north is a lighthouse on the island of Muckle Flugga. ☐ True ☐ False
5. The widest part of Scotland's mainland measures 350 miles. ☐ True ☐ False
6. The northernmost point of the Scottish mainland is John O'Groats. ☐ True ☐ False
7. Bears used to live in Scotland. ☐ True ☐ False
8. Britain's tallest tree can be found in Perthshire. ☐ True ☐ False
9. Scotland's highest mountain is 1,309m high. ☐ True ☐ False
10. Scotland's hottest day was recorded at Dumfries. ☐ True ☐ False

ANSWERS: 1. False – it is over 30,000 square miles. 2. True. 3. True. 4. True. 5. False – the widest part is 154 miles. 6. False – it is Dunnet Head. 7. True – bears lived in Scotland up to the 10th century. 8. True – the Douglas Fir measures 213 feet tall. 9. False – Ben Nevis is 1,343m high. 10. True – a record temperature of 32.8C was measured on July 2, 1908.

Spot The Differences

There are at least 15 differences between these two pictures. How many can you find?

Tom – Ouch! I've scalded my hand in the hot water.
Tim – Why didn't you feel the water before you put your hand in it?

What do you get when you cross a rabbit with a spider?
A harenet!

Minnie – I woke up last night with the feeling that my watch was gone. So I got out of bed and looked everywhere for it.
Dad – And was the watch gone?
Minnie -No, but it was going!

What falls but never gets hurt?
Snow!

Knock! Knock!
Who's there?
Noah.
Noah who?
Noah good place to eat?

Patient – I keep seeing double, doctor.
Doctor – Lie down on the couch then.
Patient – Which one?

What do you get if you cross an elephant with a fish?
A pair of swimming trunks!

Fred – Did you know that Columbus was crooked?
Jack – No, he wasn't.
Fred – He was. He double-crossed the ocean.

Commanding officer (to raw recruit) – Now, my man, I want you to regard the regiment as a big band of brothers and me as the father of the regiment. Do you understand?
Recruit – Yes, Dad.

What did the pencil say to the rubber?
Take me to your ruler!

When is an artist dangerous?
When he draws a gun!

Driving instructor – Now, young man, this is the gear lever; down there is the brake; yonder is the accelerator, and over here is the clutch.
Pupil – Let's take one thing at a time – teach me to drive first.

Visitor – What's wrong with that dog of yours? Every time I take a drink of water he growls.
Tommy – Oh, he won't bother you. He's just annoyed because you're drinking out of his cup.

Prison visitor – And what brought you here?

Prisoner – Competition.
Prison visitor – Competition?
Prisoner – Yes, I made the same kind of banknotes as the Government.

Why did Smiffy take a ladder to school?
Because he wanted to go to High School!

Patient – Doctor, doctor, I feel like a pencil.
Doctor – Can we get to the point?

Why did the Gingerbread Man wear trousers?
Because he had crummy legs!

How do fish call their friends?
By tele-fin.

Which three letters of the alphabet do all the work?
N.R.G.!

Doctor – What you need is a change of occupation. Your present job seems to be making you unhappy. What do you do?
Patient – I'm a joke writer.

Comedian – The last time I was on the stage, the people were heard laughing a mile away.
Producer – Really? What was going on there?

These eagle pictures may all look alike, but only two of them are exactly the same.
Can you spot them?

EAGLE-EYED!

A

B

C

D

E

F

WATER LOT OF FUN

Design a label for your very own brand of Scottish spring water.

Spot The Differences

There are at least 10 differences between these two pictures. How many can you find?

ADD A LETTER

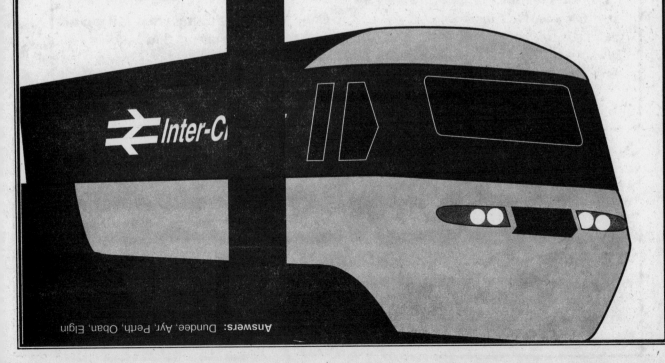

NUNUFE
NYP
FCRTII
UAAN
FLEIII

These Scottish place names on the timetable board all have lines missing. Can you add them to find the five destinations?

Inter-C

Visitor (to little boy) – If you had twelve apples, and I gave you two, how many would you have?

Little boy – I don't know. We do our sums in oranges.

Guide – Beneath that slab lies King Richard's heart; over there lies good Sir Frances Drake; and who do you think is lying here?

Tourist – Well, I don't know for sure, but I have my suspicions.

Baldheaded circus performer – Ladies and gentlemen, I offer £100 to anyone who can name anything I can't do.

Voice (from the audience) – Part your hair, in the middle!

Manager – Come here at once, John. Look at the dust on this desk. Why can't you keep it polished like the banister rails?

Office junior – Well, sir, I can't slide down your desk.

Farmer –Did you count the pigs this morning, Paddy?

Paddy – I counted nineteen, but one ran so fast that I couldn't count him at all.

Customer – You said the tortoise I bought from you would live three hundred years, and it died the day after I bought it.

Dealer – Now, isn't that too bad! The three hundred years must have been up.

Patient – How much is it to have a tooth extracted?

Dentist – Thirty pounds.

Patient – What! For three seconds' work?

Dentist – All right, I'll take it out in slow motion.

Mother – Why are you jumping up and down, Minnie?

Minnie – It's all right, Mother. I forgot to shake my medicine before I took it, so I'm doing it now.

Patient (in asylum yard, to new superintendent) – Who are you?

Superintendent – I'm the new superintendent.

Patient – Oh, it won't take them long to knock that out of you. I was Napoleon when I came here.

First gardener – What was the last card I dealt you?

Second gardener – A spade.

First gardener – I knew it.

Second gardener – How?

First gardener – You spat on your hands before you picked it up.

Teacher – Tommy, what is one-fifth of three-seventeenths?

Tommy – I don't know exactly, but it isn't enough to worry about.

Boss – What do you mean by taking the whole day off yesterday, when I gave you a half day?

Clerk – Well, you always told me never to do things by halves.

Willie – I lost a pound coin this morning, Tim.

Tim – Hole in your pocket?

Willie -No, the man who dropped it heard it fall.

Chief – We must dismiss that salesman who tells all our clients that I am an ass.

Partner – I'll speak to him, and tell him not to discuss company secrets.

Steward (to seasick passenger) – Can I fetch you anything, sir?

Seasick passenger – Yes, a small island – quick!

Angry customer – These eggs aren't fresh.

Grocer (indignantly) – Not fresh? Well, sir, the boy only brought them in from the country this morning.

Customer – Which country?

Spot The Differences

There are at least 8 differences between these two pictures. How many can you find?

ALL CHANGE!

Change one letter in each of the following words to find five favourite foods?

WINCE  PIT

SHIPS FIST

HURRY

Colouring fun

Colour this picture with your pencils or pens.

Spot The Differences

There are at least 10 differences between these two pictures. How many can you find?

Fat Fred – What? Four pounds for a shave? Your sign says two pounds!
Barber – That's right, but you've got a double chin!

Boy to teacher wearing dark glasses – Why do you wear these glasses?
Teacher – Because my pupils are very bright!

Tourist at the edge of high cliff – Don't you think there should be a warning sign here? It's a very dangerous cliff!
Tour guide – They did have one, but nobody fell over so they took it down!

Fatty – I'm going to grow a moustache and beard when I grow up.
Wilfrid – Why?
Fatty – So that I won't have so much face to wash.

Baker – Good morning, madam. Bread's gone up another penny today.
Mrs Hardup – Oh, has it? Well, give me a yesterday's loaf.

Captain – Let's find out just how much you know about a boat. What would you do if a sudden storm sprang up on the starboard?
Danny – Throw out the anchor.
Captain – What would you do if another storm sprang up aft?
Danny – Throw out another anchor.
Captain – And if another storm sprang up forward, what would you do?
Danny – Throw out another anchor.
Captain – Hold on. Where are you getting all your anchors from?
Danny – From the same place you're getting your storms.

Gamekeeper – Don't you know you're not allowed to fish here?
Sandy – I'm not fishing. I'm teaching a worm to swim!

Waiter – How did you find your steak?
Diner – Easy. I'm a detective!

Tim – My Dad's got a leading position in a circus!
Tom – Gosh! What does he do?
Tim – He leads in the elephants!

Danny – Why are you looking at the mirror with your eyes shut?
'Erbert – I want to see what I look like when I'm asleep.

How did the witch know she wasn't well?
She had a dizzy spell.

Diner – Waiter, waiter, there's a spider in my soup.
Waiter – Oh, yes, sir. All the flies are on holiday.

Teacher – Toots, can you name the four seasons?
Toots – Yes, sir! Salt, mustard, vinegar and pepper!

Mother – What's wrong, Smiffy? Did something fall on your head?
Smiffy – Y-yes. I did!

Policeman (to boy looking over the wall of the football stadium) – Hey, what's the game?
Bobby – Football. Rovers versus United!

Teacher (in a Glasgow school) – Do you know the population of Glasgow?
Jimmy – Not all of them. I've only been here a week!

Dad – Harold, you mustn't go fishing with the boy next door – he's just had measles.
Harold – Oh, it's all right, Dad. I never catch anything when I go fishing.

What's the longest night of the year?
A fortnight!

What is the longest word in the English language?
Smile – because there's a mile in it.

Spot The Differences

There are at least 10 differences between these two pictures. How many can you find?

Spot The Differences

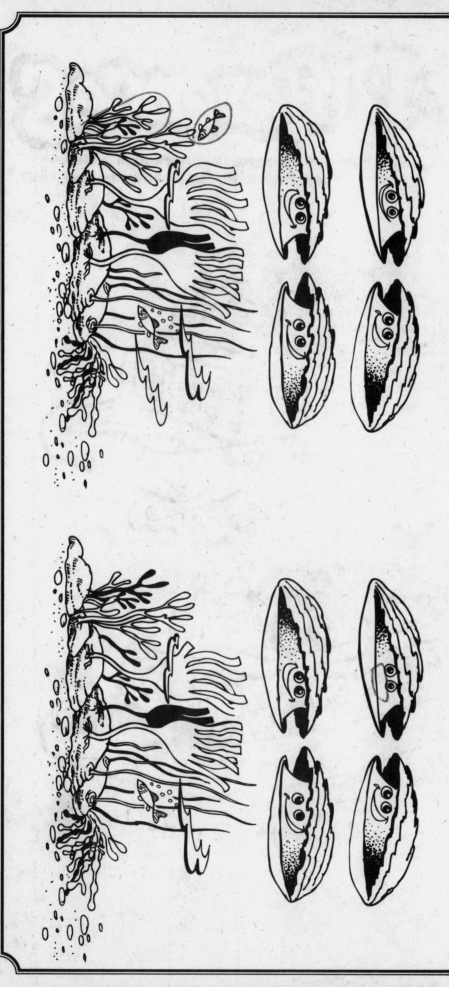

There are at least 8 differences between these two pictures. How many can you find?

Weary Willie – Why don't you look for work?
Lazy Len – I'm afraid.
Weary Willie – Of what?
Lazy Len – Finding it!

Bill – Have you heard that they're not making lampposts any longer?
David – Why?
Bill – They're long enough already.

Freddie – My brother has taken up French, Italian, Spanish and Greek.
Old man – Goodness! What does he do?
Freddie – He's a lift boy.

Headmaster – I don't see why you're grumbling. This is splendid tea.
Teacher – Yes, sir, but Olive, the dinner lady, says it's soup!

Young girl – Please, Mother says will you give me the broom you borrowed last Thursday?
Neighbour – Yes, but don't forget to bring it back.

Sidney – How many pieces of that toffee do I get for fifty pence?
Shop assistant – Oh, two or three.
Sidney – I'll take three, please.

Danny – What do you think you're talking about?
Cuthbert – I don't think – I know.
Danny – I don't think you know either.

How's business?
I manage to keep my head above water.
Well, wood floats, you know.

'Erbert – Mother Nature is wonderful! A million years ago she didn't know we were going to wear spectacles, yet look at the way she placed our ears.

What lives under the sea and carries sixty-four people?
An octobus!

Teacher – Dennis, what do we call a person who is very talkative, yet uninteresting?
Dennis – A teacher.

An absent-minded professor went into a shop to buy a jar. Seeing one upside down, he said, "How stupid, this jar has no mouth!" Turning it over, he was more astonished. "Why, there's no bottom in it, either!"

Patient – Doctor, doctor, I think I'm shrinking!
Doctor – Well, you'll just have to be a little patient.

When did the Scottish potato change its nationality?
When it became a French fry!

Two flies were on Robinson Crusoe's head. "Goodbye for now," said one. "I'll see you on Friday!"

What do you call a man who breaks into a meat factory?
A hamburglar!

Teacher – Why have you got cotton wool in your ear? Is it infected?
Smiffy – No, sir, but you said yesterday that everything you told me went in one ear and out the other, so I'm trying to stop it.

Where do pigs play?
In a play-pork!

What kind of monkeys make the best wine?
Grey apes.

Why is a game of cricket like a pancake?
Because they both depend on a good batter.

Who tells chicken jokes?
Comedihens!

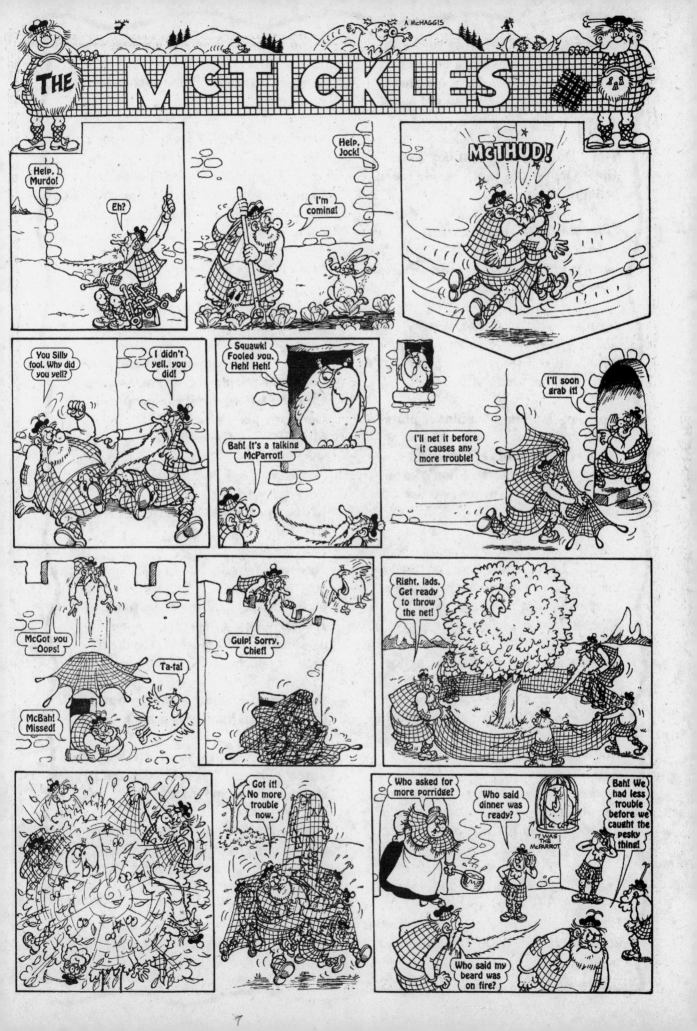

Busy greengrocer (who has gone into next-door shop, which is a beauty parlour) – Will you massage those prunes for me, please, miss? We've run out of plums.

Tim – Do you know that boy Jones?
Jim – Oh, yes, he sleeps beside me in history.

Little brother – What's etiquette?
Slightly bigger brother – It's saying "No, thank you!" at a birthday party when you want to say "Yes, please!"

Dennis – What's the time, Walter?
Walter – Twenty-five minutes to ten.
Dennis – I'll never remember that. You'd better give me your watch.

Optician (holding up a dinner plate) – What is this?
'Erbert (getting his eyes tested) – Bring it a little nearer. I don't know whether it's a five pence or a ten pence.

Teacher (after looking at Smiffy's home-work) – I didn't think it was possible for one person to make so many mistakes.
Smiffy – It wasn't only one person, Teacher. Dad helped me.

Gentleman – Are you still looking for your lost pound coin, little boy?
Boy – No, my little brother found it.
Gentleman – Then what are you looking for?
Boy – My little brother.

Mother – Why didn't you take the medicine the doctor gave you for your cold?
Minnie – Because it says on the bottle, "Keep tightly corked."

Poet – This poem of mine will make everybody's heart miss a beat.
Editor – Then it won't do. We never print anything that interferes with the circulation.

Pupil – I can't read this correction of yours, sir.
Teacher – It says, "You must write more clearly."

First weightlifter – I am stronger than Hercules.
Second weightlifter – That's nothing. I knew a man who could pick himself up by the scruff of the neck and swing himself out at arm's length.

Bill – How long did you work last week?
Ben – One day.
Bill – Gosh! I wish I could find a steady job like that.

Teacher – The people of Poland are Poles; the people of Sweden, Swedes. Can you tell me what the people of Germany are called?
Minnie – Yes, Germs.

Foreman – Look how that man's doing twice the work you are.
Workman – That's what I've been telling him, but he won't stop.

Teacher – Why are you late this morning?
Jock – Please, sir, I stopped a fight.
Teacher – That's right, always be a peacemaker. How did you stop them?
Jock – I punched them both.

Novice (hiring boat) – I've no watch so I hope I shall know when my hour is up.
Boatman – Oh, yes, you'll know by the water. The boat fills up to the seat in about an hour and a half.

Diner – I ordered a dozen oysters, and you've only given me eleven.
Waiter – I thought you wouldn't like to sit thirteen at the table, sir.

Confused judge (to noisy prisoner in court) – Quiet please! We want nothing but silence, and very little of that.

Draw suitable pictures for the front of these holiday postcards.

Edinburgh - Scotland's Capital

St Andrews - Home of golf

Spot The Differences

There are at least 6 differences between these two pictures. How many can you find?

Spot the Differences

There are at least 8 differences between these two pictures. How many can you find?

Why did the sailor grab a piece of soap when he was sinking?
So he could wash himself ashore.

What are the best kind of letters to read in hot weather?
Fan mail!

What is out of bounds?
An exhausted kangaroo!

Wife – Doctor, doctor, my husband's broken his leg.
Doctor – But madam, I'm a doctor of music.
Wife – That's all right, it was the piano that fell on him!

What do you call a toffee train?
A chew chew!

What do you give a deaf fisherman?
A herring aid?

What birds are cowboys afraid of?
Toma-hawks.

Why is Cinderella such a rotten footballer?
Because her coach is a pumpkin!

What did the Mona Lisa say to the gallery attendant?
I've been framed!

What is short, green and goes camping?
A boy sprout!

Eck – Why wouldn't they let the butterfly into the dance?
Bob – Because it was a moth ball!

How should you dress on a cold day?
Quickly!

Doctor, my husband thinks he's a clothes line.
Bring him round to the surgery.
What, and have all my washing fall on the ground?

Ticket collector – Are you first class?
Second-class passenger – Oh, yes, I'm fine, thank you. How's yourself?

Knock! Knock!
Who's there?
Senor.
Senor who?
Senor father out and let me in!

Why is a fish shop always crowded?
Because the fish fillet!

Boastful angler – I once had a three-hour fight with a salmon.
Bored friend – Yes, tin openers can be a nuisance at times.

Landlady – I don't allow cats, dogs, radios or record players in my house!
New lodger – Er … do you mind if my shoes squeak a little?

Teacher – What happens to gold when it is exposed to the air?
Smiffy – It's stolen!

Mrs McDougall – I want a pair of fur gloves!
Assistant – Yes, madam. What fur?
Mrs McDougall – What fur? To keep my hands warm, of course!

Father – Sidney, are you tall enough to reach that package on the mantelpiece?
Sidney – Not if it's my cough mixture!

Diner – I find that I have just enough money to pay the dinner, but I have nothing left to give you a tip.
Waiter – Let me add up that bill again, sir.

Farmer to man – If you can guess how many chickens I have, I'll give you both of them!

What do you get when you cross a sparrow with a haddock?
Cheep fish.

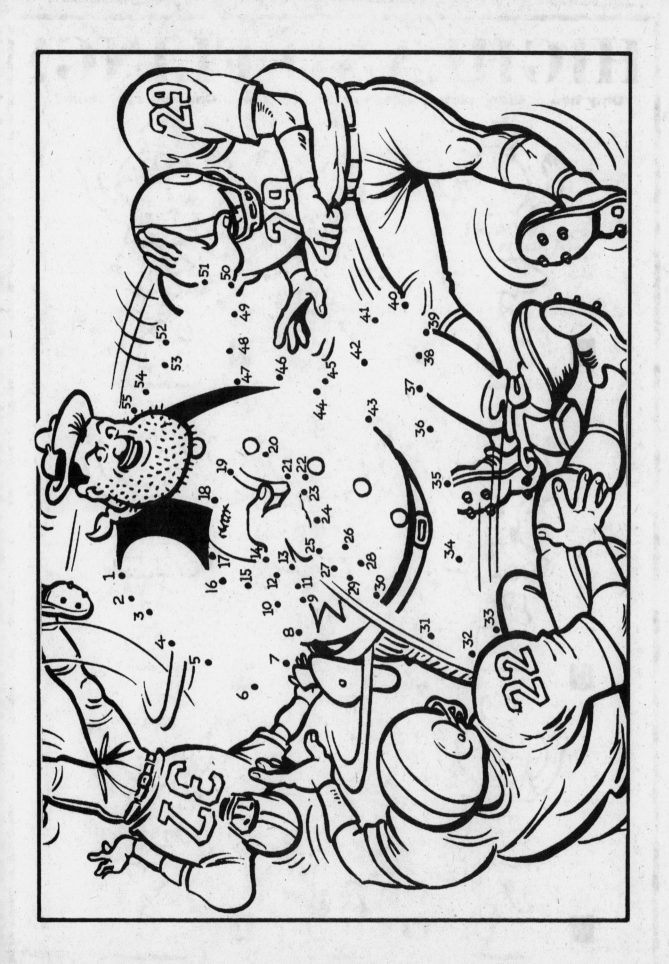

HIGHLAND FLING!

Only two of these pictures are exactly the same. Can you spot them?

A   B   C

D   E   F

G   H   I

The Jocks and the Geordies

 ANGUS
 HECTOR
 SANDY
 WEE ECK
 BIG JOCK
 SIDNEY
 CEDRIC
 EGBERT
 ARNOLD
 LANKY

Danny – Why do you call your new dog Ginger?
Sidney – Because he snaps!

Brring! Brring!
Who's there?
Hurd.
Hurd who?
Hurd my hand, so couldn't Knock!
Knock!

Smiffy – I went to the dentist yesterday.
Toots – Does your tooth still hurt?
Smiffy – I don't know – the dentist kept it.

First tramp – I have heard of a million-aire who wears a suit of clothes only once.
Second tramp – So do we, but it's a longer once.

Teacher – What is the name of the pine with the longest and sharpest needles?
Danny – The porcupine.

Fisherman – Do the fish in this river bite?
Gamekeeper – Bite? They're so fierce that you have to hide behind a tree while you are baiting your hook.

Minnie – There's something without any legs running across the yard.
Dad – What is it?
Minnie – Water. You left the tap on.

Smith – Did I leave an umbrella here yesterday?
Restaurant manager – What kind of umbrella?
Smith – Oh, any kind. I'm not particular.

Wilfrid – Why does it rain, Dad?
Dad – To make the grass grow.
Wilfrid – Then why does it rain on the streets?

Who became a space hero by mistake?
Fluke Skywalker.

Teacher – If you use this text book, you will get your homework done in half the time.
Danny – Great! Can I have two?

Teacher – Brian, how old were you on your last birthday?
Brian – Seven, Miss.
Teacher – Very good! That means you'll be eight on your next birthday.
Brian – No, Miss. I'll be nine!
Teacher – But that's impossible!
Brian – No it isn't. I'm eight today, Miss!

Danny – What has ten legs, a yellow back, a green eye and a long, horned tail?
Cuthbert – I don't know.

Danny – Neither do I, but I've just seen one swimming in your soup!

Plug – What is black and white and red all over?
Teacher – I know that one, Plug, a news-paper!
Plug – No sir, a zebra with a sun tan!

Boss – So you can do anything? Can you wheel a barrow full of smoke?
Workman – Yes, if you fill it for me.

Lazy Larry – Well, here I am to see about the job you advertised.
Contractor – Oh, do you think you are fit to work?
Lazy Larry – Work? I thought you wanted a foreman!

Why are you running?
There's a lion loose.
Which way did it go?
Do you think I'm following it?

Speaker – How long have I been speak-ing? I haven't got a watch with me.
Danny – There's a calendar behind you.

Teacher – What is meant by extrava-gance?
Sidney – Wearing a tie below a beard.

Spot The Differences

There are at least 10 differences between these two pictures. How many can you find?

Spot The Differences

There are at least 10 differences between these two pictures. How many can you find?

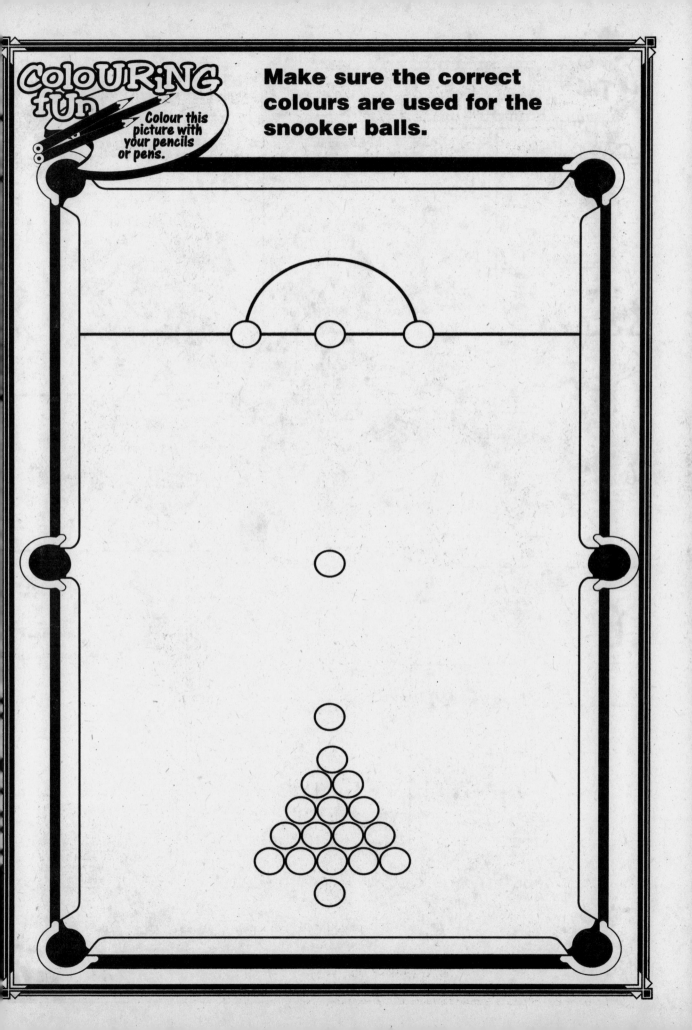

ColoURiNG fUn

Colour this picture with your pencils or pens.

Make sure the correct colours are used for the snooker balls.

WATCH THE BIRDIE!

These owls may look alike but one is different.

A

B

C

D

Uncle – What are you looking so worried about, Jack?
Young Nephew – Well, yesterday my teacher said two and two are four, and today Dad said one and three are four, and I don't know which to believe.

Which driver never commits a traffic offence?
A screwdriver!

What can you hold without touching it?
A conversation.

Hotel manager – Rooms overlooking the sea cost £5 extra.
Miser – How much does it cost if I promise not to look?

David – If you call somebody who lives in Scotland Scottish, what do you call somebody who lives in the North Pole?
Tom – I don't know!
David – Daft!

Bill – How do you confuse a boomerang?
Ben – I don't know!
Bill – Throw it down a one-way street!

Officer – Have you cleaned your boots this morning?
Private – No.
Officer – No, what?
Private – No polish.

Dad – What's the time?
Dennis – Half past.
Dad – Half past what?
Dennis – I dunno. I've lost the hour hand of my watch!

Alec – What was your mother so angry about?
Jim – She sent me for some cold cream and I got ice-cream. It was the coldest they had.

Teacher – If you had twelve sweets, and Johnny took half, what would he have?
Tommy – A black eye!

Fireman – Hey! Come on! Can't you see your house is on fire?
Patient – Can't help it. The doctor told me not to leave my bed for two days.

Diner – There's a funny kind of film on this soup, waiter.
Waiter – Well, what do you expect for two pounds – a full-scale thriller?

Youth – Shall I have a chance of an early rise in this job?
Boss – Most certainly! Six o'clock every morning.

Boss – I want a man who is clever, hard-working and punctual.
Lazy Larry – You don't want one man, you want three.

Teacher – If you had two pounds and you asked your dad for another two pounds, how much money would you have?
Johnny – Er … two pounds, sir.

Where do old Volkswagens go?
The Old Volks' Home!

When a fly from one side of the room and a flea from the other side meet, what is the time when they pass?
Fly-past-flea!

Doctor, doctor, I keep on getting a sore throat every time I take a cup of tea.
Doctor – Have you tried taking the spoon out.

Which land do kittens like best?
Lapland!

What do you call a map-reading back-seat driver?
A nag-ivator!

Boss – What do you mean by arguing with that customer? Don't you know our rule? The customer is always right.
Assistant – I know. But he was insisting that he was wrong.

Little Willie – Gran, was Dad a very bad boy when he was small?
Gran – Why?
Little Willie – Because he knows exactly what questions to ask when he wants to know what I've been doing.

Mother – Dennis, what are you reading?
Dennis – I don't know, Mum.
Mother – But you were reading aloud.
Dennis – I know, but I wasn't listening.

What did the rocket's door say?
Gone to launch!

Teacher – Sidney, what is that swelling on your nose?
Sidney – I bent down to smell a brose, sir.
Teacher – There's no "B" in rose, Sidney.
Sidney – There was in this one.

What is the fastest liquid in the world?
Milk, because it is pasteurised before you see it.

Paperboy – Special! Read all about it. Forty-nine people swindled!
McSporran – I don't see anything here about a swindle.
Paperboy- Special! Read all about it! Fifty people swindled.

'Erbert – How do you spell blind pig?
Wilfrid – Easy – B.L.I.N.D. P.I.G.
'Erbert – Wrong! B.L.N.D. P.G.
Wilfrid – Why is that?
'Erbert – Because if it had two "I"s it wouldn't be a blind pig.

McGraw – How old is old Archie?
McGill – I dunno, but everybody was overcome by the heat from his candles at his last birthday party.

Doctor – Now take a deep breath and say nine three times.
Smart Alec (after inhaling) – Twenty-seven!

Frankie – Please, Mrs Smart, is Bobby coming out to play?
Mrs Smart – No, Frankie, it's too wet.
Frankie – Well, is his football coming out, then?

Bob – With patience, you can do anything.
Bill – Can I fill this sieve with water?
Bob – Yes, if you wait till it freezes.

Teacher – Now, Billy, what letter in the alphabet comes before "J"?
Billy – I dunno.
Teacher – What have I on both sides of my nose?
Billy – Freckles.

Judge – You are sentenced to ten years' imprisonment. Have you anything to add?
Prisoner – No, but I'd like to subtract.

Doctor – Have you taken the box of pills I gave you?
Oswald – Yes, but I feel worse. Perhaps the cardboard disagreed with me.

Mrs Perkins – Have you eaten these sandwiches?
Mr Perkins – Yes.
Mrs Perkins – Well, you'll have to clean your shoes with meat paste, for I put the boot polish on the sandwiches by mistake.

Policeman – I arrested a man for stealing a calendar yesterday!
Joe – What did he get?
Policeman – Twelve months!

If "L" on a car means learner, what does "GB" mean?
Getting better.

Why is a baby like a diamond?
Because it's such a dear little thing.

What sort of fish sings songs?
Tuna fish.

One of these ladybirds is different from the others. Can you spot it?

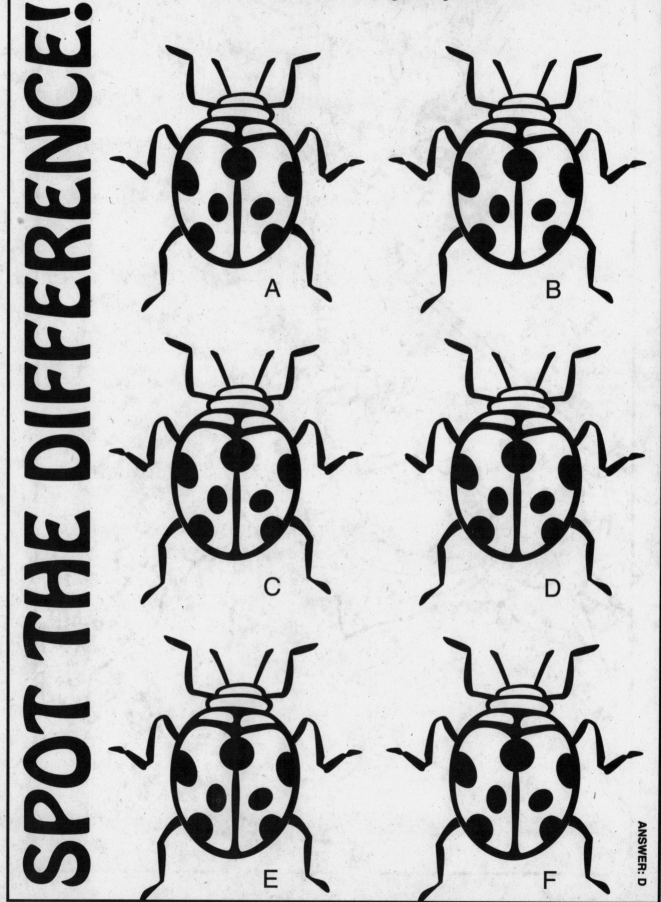

SPOT THE DIFFERENCE!

A B C D E F

Western Isles

How to put together your Scottish Map colouring poster.

Carefully tear out this page and the following eight poster pages. Then carefully finish trimming the pages by cutting along the dotted lines.

Paste the strip at the edge of the sheet B as shown, then place A in position to match the pictures together. Do the same with sheets B and C. Now join sheets D, E and F and then G, H and I in the same way.

Next paste the strips of the attached sheets D, E and F. Stick down the sheets A, B and C to match the pictures together then do the same with sheets G, H and I. If you like you can make your poster stronger by turning it over and taping the edges together. Now you're ready to colour your poster.

Ask an adult to help you if you are not sure how to put this poster together.

C	B	A
F	E	D
I	H	G

BACK OF POSTER

HIGHLAND

Moray

B

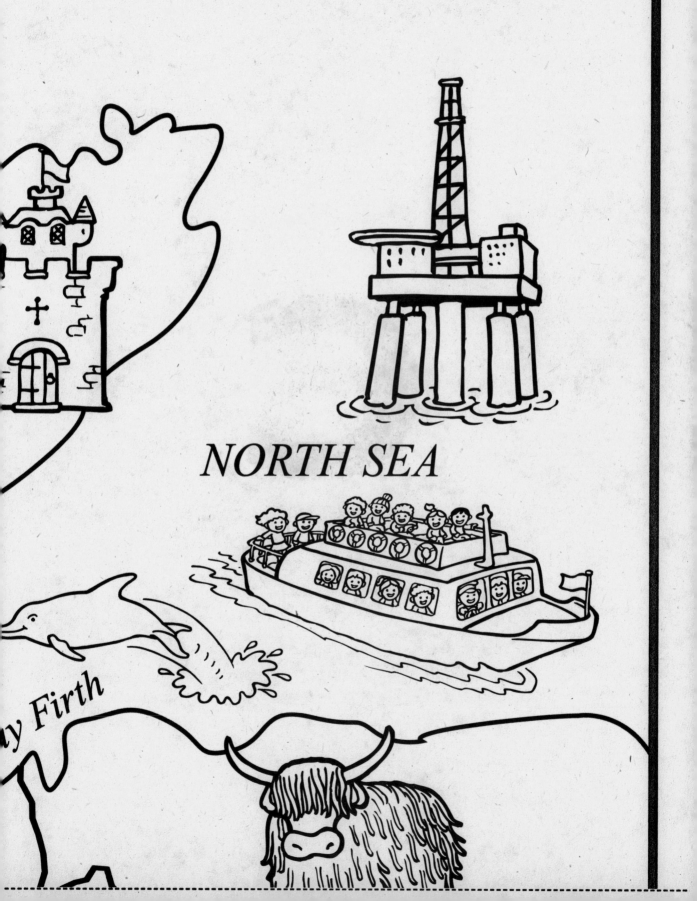

NORTH SEA

Firth

PASTE ↑B PASTE

TA

CENTRAL

E

GRAMPIAN

Aberdeen

'AYSIDE

Dundee

Perth

F

G

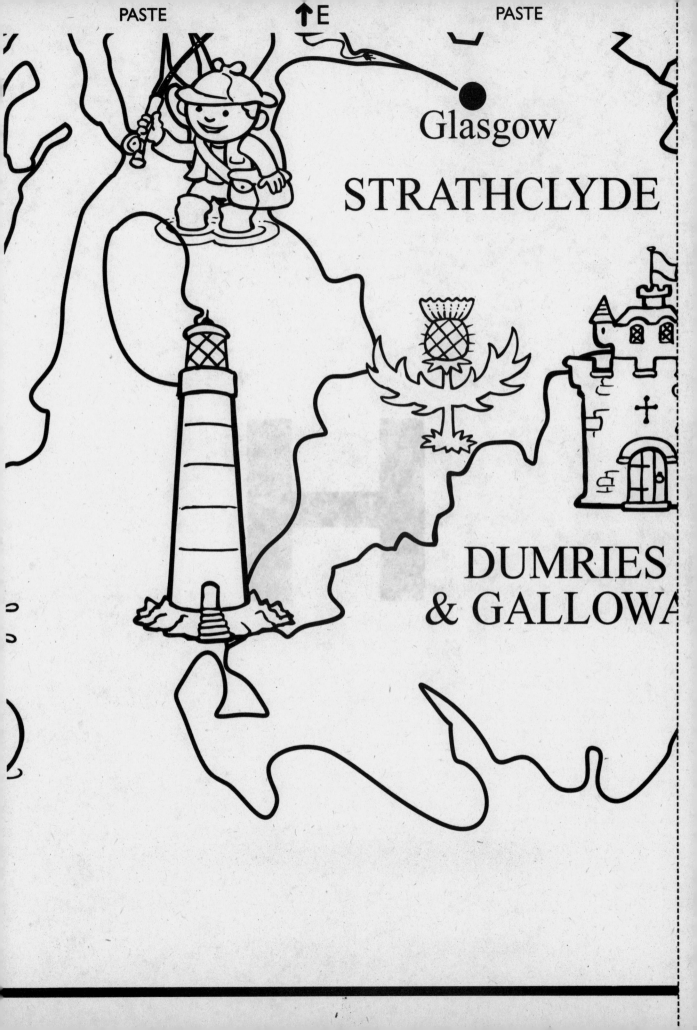

Glasgow

STRATHCLYDE

DUMRIES
& GALLOWA

H

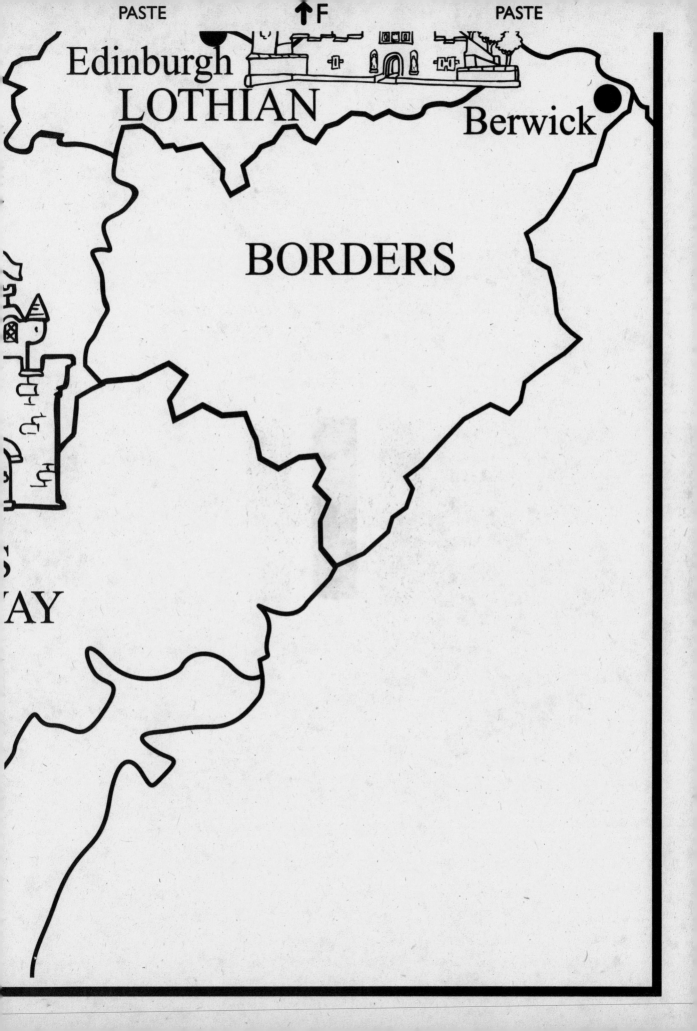

PASTE ↑F PASTE

Edinburgh

LOTHIAN

Berwick

BORDERS

AY

BRIGHT IDEAS
PLANTS, BIRDS & BOXES

Collect seeds from a selection of local plants or trees.
Next time you are in the countryside, plant them in verges or waste ground.
Your flowers will look super when they start to grow and people will be less likely to dump rubbish there.
Alternatively, you could buy a packet of mixed wild flower seeds and scatter these around. The seeds you scatter or plant may take some time to grow but the end result will be worthwhile.

Encourage wild birds to your garden by putting up a bird table and hanging bags and containers of nuts and birdfood. Soon, your garden will be filled with all sorts of feathered visitors. Remember to put out containers of water, too, because the birds will need this in summer and winter.

Birds can also be encouraged to visit your garden if you put up nest boxes for them and you can encourage nocturnal visitors such as Pipistrelles by putting up a bat box.

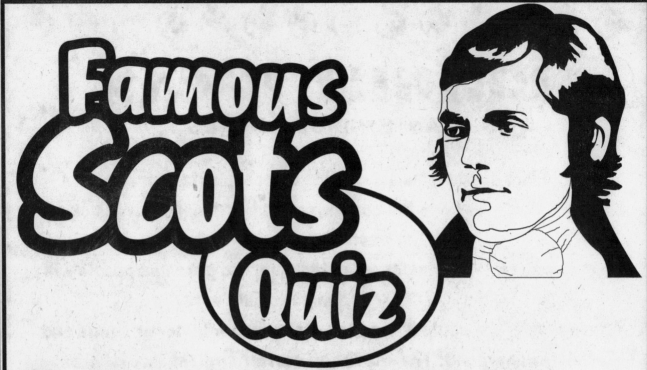

Famous Scots Quiz

1. Which famous Scot played the voice of Draco the Dragon in the film Dragonheart?

2. Who won twenty seven Formula One races and three World Championships?

3. Which famous Scot wrote Peter Pan?

4. Who sailed to America at the age to twelve and later became the "father of the US navy"?

5. Who created the first pneumatic tyre?

6. Which Scot's born inventor was responsible for the telephone, the tetrahedron and the hydro foil?

7. Which famous Scottish poet wrote about a haggis and a mouse?

8. Which native of Glasgow was the inventor of the first rain jacket?

9. The life of which famous Scottish hero was dramatised in the film "Braveheart"?

10. Which Scot born in Glasgow donated a huge collection of over 8000 items of art and antiques to the city?

ANSWERS 1. Sean Connery, 2. Jackie Stewart; 3. Sir James Barrie; 4. John Paul Jones; 5. John Boyd Dunlop; 6. Alexander Graham Bell; 7. Robert Burns; 8. Charles Macintosh; 9. Sir William Wallace; 10. Sir William Burrell.

SPOT THE BIRDIE

Which of these birds is the odd one out?

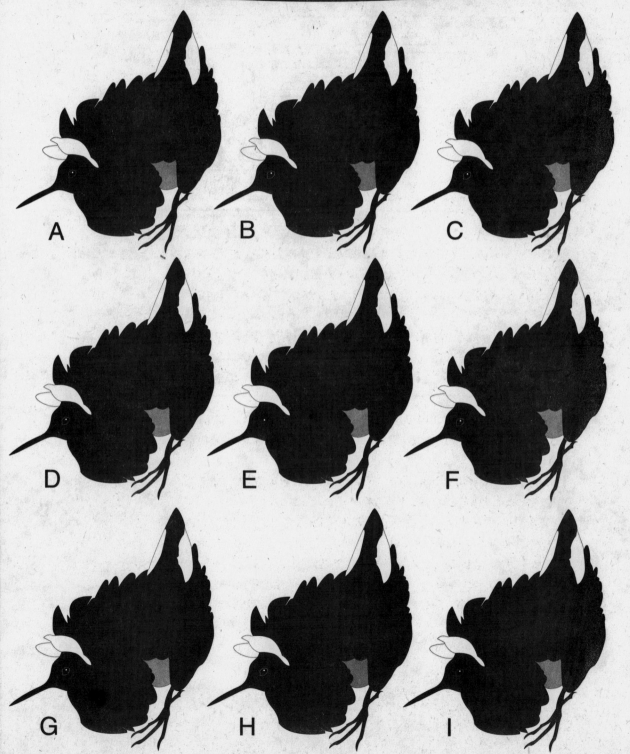

A   B   C

D   E   F

G   H   I

the Jocks and the Geordies

 ANGUS HECTOR SANDY WEE ECK BIG JOCK SIDNEY CEDRIC EBBERT ARNOLD LANKY

CABER CRAZY

Two of these figures tossing the caber are exactly the same. Can you spot them?

A

B

C

D

E

F

SPOT THE BIRDIE

These birds may look alike, but only two of them are exactly the same. Can you spot them?

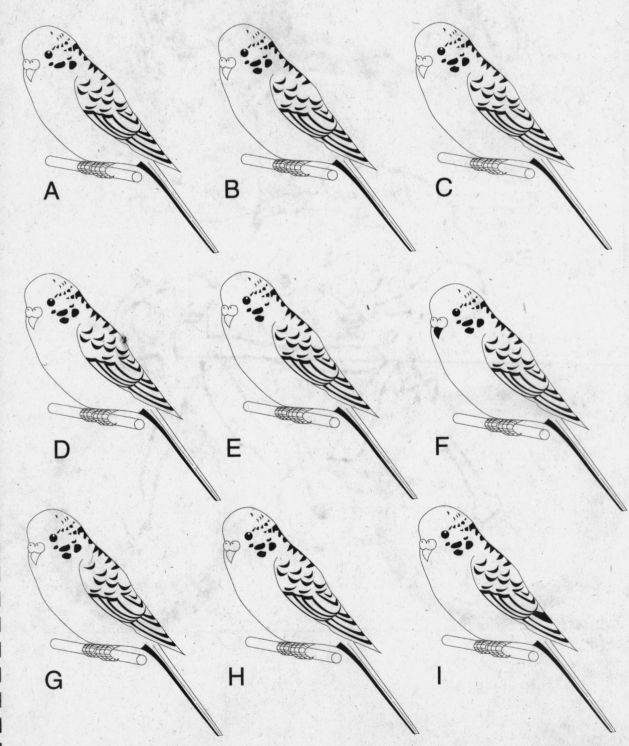

A

B

C

D

E

F

G

H

I

SPOT THE BIRDIE

Which of these bird pictures is the odd one out?

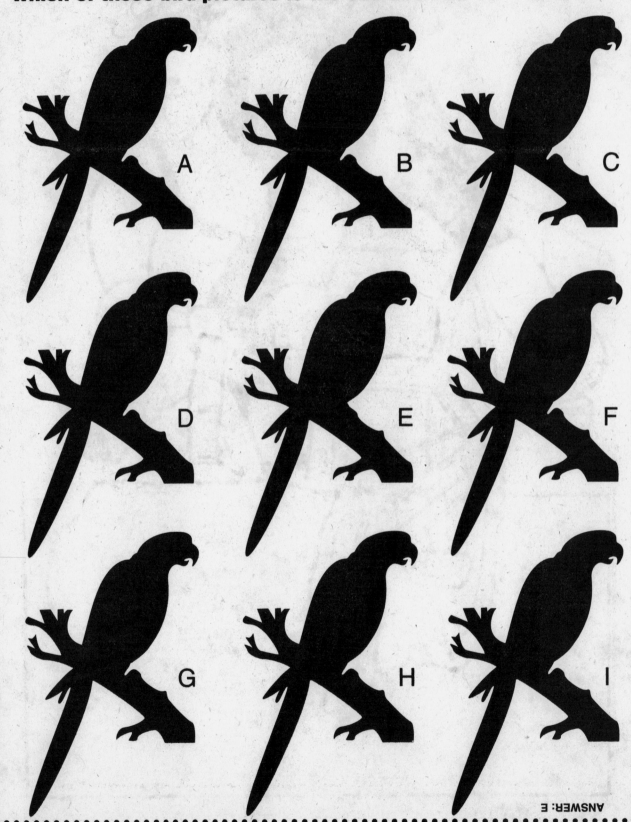

A

B

C

D

E

F

G

H

I

What vegetable is green and strong?
A muscle sprout.

Plug – I saw something last night that I'll never get over.
Danny – What was that?
Plug – The moon!

Diner – I say, waiter, bring my hat.
Waiter – It's on your head, sir.
Diner -Then don't bother. I'll look for it myself.

Smiffy – I wish I'd lived at the very beginning of the world.
Toots – Why?
Smiffy – Because I wouldn't have had to learn history.

It was my wife's birthday yesterday, so I bought her a rocket.
Was she delighted?
Yes, over the moon.

What was awarded to the inventor of door knockers?
The No-bell prize!

Mum – What are you doing, Tommy?
Tommy – I'm writing a letter to my sister.
Mum – Don't be silly, you can't write.
Tommy – That doesn't matter, she can't read.

Patient – Doctor, my family think I'm a little odd.
Doctor – Why?
Patient – Because I like sausages.
Doctor – Nonsense. I like sausages too.
Patient – You do? You must come round to see my collection. I have hundreds.

Danny – I have a great memory. I can recite all the names on five pages of the telephone directory.
Wifrid – I don't believe you!
Danny – Right then – Smith, Smith, Smith, Smith, Smith …

Why did you give up singing in the choir?
I was ill last week and didn't go, and after the service someone asked if the organ had been mended.

Angler (telling tall story) – Yes, the fish I caught was so big that I simple couldn't pull it out of the water.
Sarcastic listener – It was a whale, I suppose?
Angler – A whale? Goodness, no! I was baiting with whales.

Diner – Waiter, this bread has got sand on it.
Waiter – Yes, sir, it helps to keep the butter from sliding off.

What is white and goes up?
A stupid snowflake!

Grandpa – How long have you been going to school, Angus?
Angus – Too . . .
Grandpa – Two years?
Angus – No, too long.

Auntie – Do you ever help your little brother, Andrew?

Andrew – Yes, Auntie, I helped him to spend the five pounds you gave him yesterday!

What do you get if you cross a chip shop with a famous train?
The Frying Scotsman!

The new bank clerk's hobby is climbing trees.
He must want to be a branch manager!

Knock, knock!
Who's there?
The Invisible Man.
Tell him I can't see him at the moment!

What are the two fastest fish in the sea?
A motor pike and a side carp!

Pony Puzzler

Look carefully. Can you find the picture that is different from the rest?

The Jocks and the Geordies

 ANGUS HECTOR SANDY WEE ECK BIG JOCK SIDNEY CEDRIC EGBERT ARNOLD LANKY

The Geordies are out bird-watching—

BUZZ! ERK! WHASSAT? I HOPE IT'S NOT WHAT I THINK YOU THINK IT IS!

TIMBER! WAAH! HELP!

MO! MO! SUPER MO... GREAT! COUSIN MO'S A LUMBERJACK! MOAN? MOAN? OOH! WHAT HAPPENED? GROAN?

GRR! I DON'T THINK WE LIKE HIM! ...SUPER MORRIS JOCK-MAN!

CERTAINLY DON'T! WE'RE GONNA HAVE TO AVOID HIM! But— HOO! MORRIS LIKES TO KEEP FIT BY CYCLING — HE'S COOL! SPLAT! OOFYAH!

HE ALSO LIKES TO RUN ON THE SPOT! AARGH!

I'M ALSO KEEN ON MOUNTAIN-CLIMBING — HERE'S A TRICK ONE OF MY PALS SHOWED ME!

PIPER PAIR!

Only two of these six pipers are identical. Which two?

SPOT THE BIRDIE

One of these birds is completely different to the others.
Can you spot it?

A　B　C

D　E　F

G　H　I

the Jocks and the Geordies

ANGUS HECTOR SANDY WEE ECK BIG JOCK SIDNEY CEDRIC EGBERT ARNOLD LANKY

EEK! THE GEORDIES HAVE CHALLENGED US TO A GAME OF FOOTBALL.

SNORE!

C'MON, LADS! WE'VE GOT SOME SERIOUS TRAINING TO DO!

JINGS! WHIT'S THE RUSH?

PULL!

So—

COO! ARE YOU GONNA CURL THE BALL AROUND THOSE DUMMIES, BIG JOCK?

DON'T BE DAFT!

I'M TRYING TO HIT THE WALL! THAT COULD BE A GEORDIE!

OOH! GOOD SHOT THEN!

THUD!

CRASH!

NOW IT'S TIME FOR YOU TO PRACTISE YOUR HEADING, ECK!

BRILLIANT!

RUB!

HERE IT COMES!

TOSS!

LEAP!

KERRACK!

OWW!

GREAT SHOT!

YOU'RE A PROPER HEAD-BANGER, WEE ECK!

PAT!

I AM? COO, TA!

C'MON, LADS. TIME TO GET OUR BOOTS ON!

GOOD IDEA.

Gnock! Gnock!

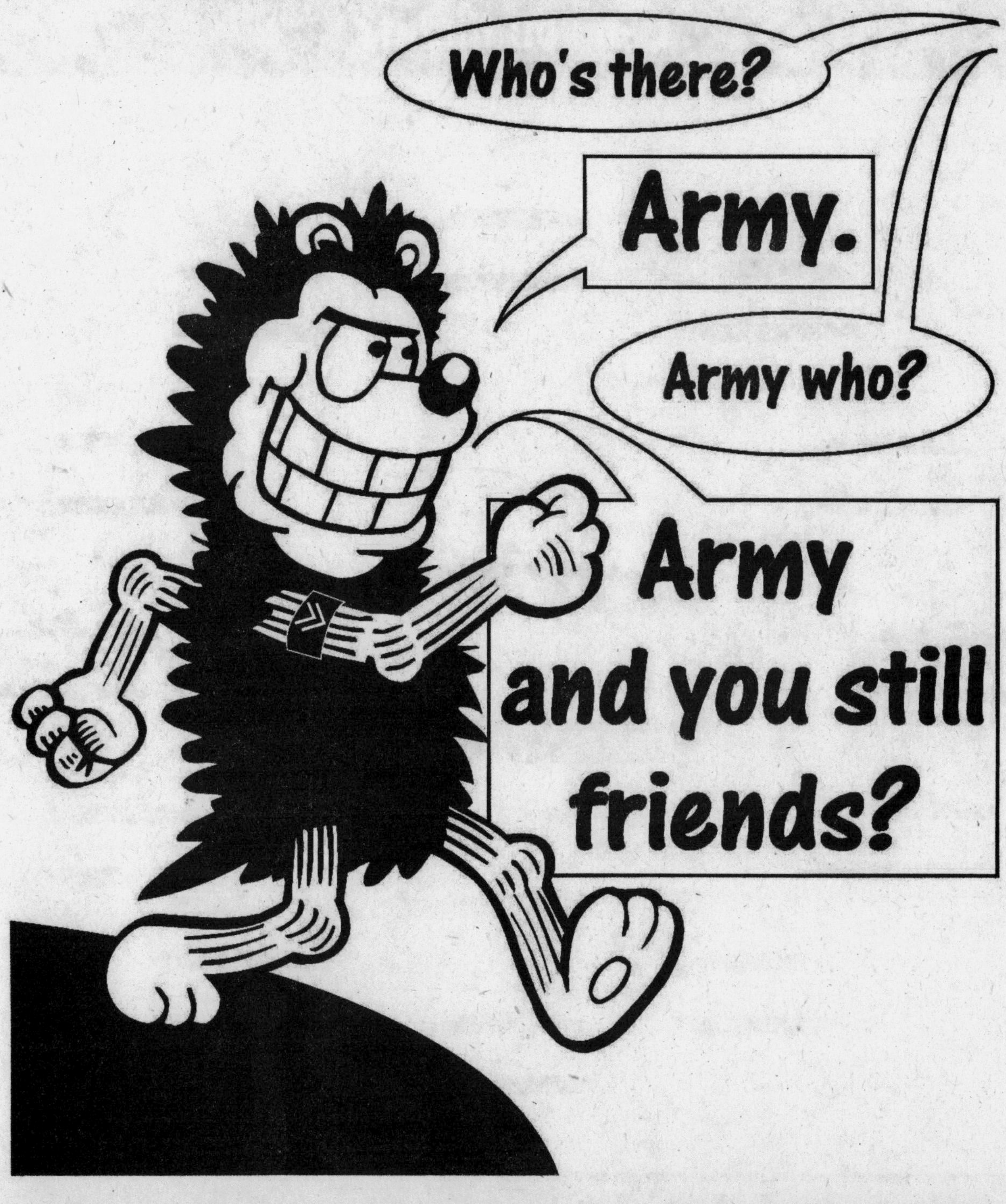

⬭ON THE ICE

These curling stones may all look alike, but only one of them matches the one in the middle. Can you find it?

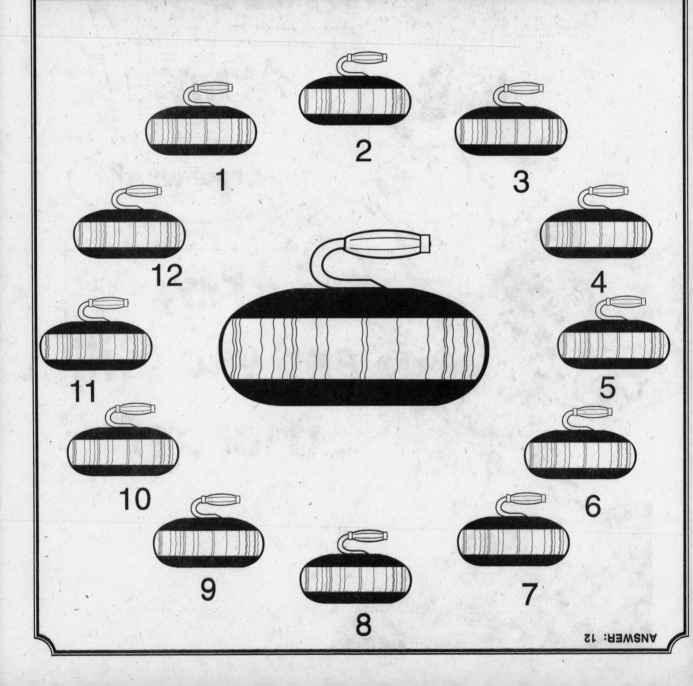

LOTS OF BROLLIES

Which of these brollies is different from the rest?

A

B

C

D

E

F

the Jocks and the Geordies

 ANGUS HECTOR SANDY WEE ECK BIG JOCK SIDNEY CEDRIC EBBERT ARNOLD LANKY

FINE EXAMPLE OF MODERN ART

BUT IS IT REALLY ART?

IT SURE IS, BOYS. I'D PAY A MILLION BUCKS FOR SOMETHING LIKE THAT!

ERK! IT'S PABLO POLONEY, THE AMERICAN MILLIONAIRE!

OKAY, LADS. YOU GO VISIT THE JOCKS AND I'LL BRING MISTER POLONEY ALONG TO SEE — ERM — WORKS OF ART.

GOOD IDEA!

So, presently—

WHEE!

Suddenly—

DIVERSION

OOPS! JUST SAW THAT SIGN IN TIME — ERK!

CRASH!

HOW ABOUT THIS, MISTER POLONEY? IT'S CALLED "CARNAGE ON WHEELS".

SORRY, KID. I AIN'T TOO KEEN ON STILL LIFES!

And—

WHIT A MATCH THAT WAS!

AYE, DID YE SEE THE PASS O' KILLIECRANKIE?

PULL! PULL!

WEAAAH!

ERK!

HEADS!

**Only two of these pictures are exactly the same.
Can you spot them?**

BRIGHT IDEAS

FUN WITH FRIENDS

?

?

? **A treasure hunt is fun. Write out a clue that will lead your friends to another hidden clue and so on until they find the treasure – sweets, a comic or an inexpensive toy are ideal. The clues can be hidden all round the house and in the garden. The final clue will lead the winner to the treasure.**

?

Pass out paper and pencils to your friends and have fun drawing quirky cartoons of each other. Have lots of laughs making your cartoons as funny as possible.

Get together with your friends to make up a secret code. You can then send each other secret messages that no one else can read. Make sure you keep a copy of the code, though, or you won't be able to find out the secrets either.

Have some of your friends for a sleepover. You can make fun-size pizzas and sandwiches to eat and take turns telling scary ghost stories. Have a prize for the person telling the scariest story.

How to put together your Scottish Shield colouring poster.

Carefully tear out this page and the following three poster pages. Then carefully finish trimming the pages by cutting along the dotted lines.

Paste the strip at the edge of the sheet A as shown, then place B in position to match the pictures together. Do the same with sheets C and D.

Next paste the strips of the attached sheets C and D. Stick down the sheets A and B to make the picture complete. If you like you can make your poster stronger by turning it over and taping the edges together. Now you're ready to colour your Scottish Shield poster.

Ask an adult to help you if you are not sure how to put this poster together.

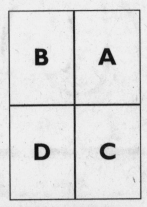

BACK OF POSTER

B

D

Gnock! Gnock!

Who's there?
Lettuce.
Lettuce who?
Lettuce out, it's cold
in here!

the Jocks and the Geordies

 ANGUS
 HECTOR
 SANDY
 WEE ECK
 BIG JOCK
 SIDNEY
 CEDRIC
 EGBERT
 ARNOLD
 LANKY

THE GEORDIES HAVE HAD THEIR SHED DECORATED.

DANDY ANNUALS

IT PUTS OUR DUMP TO SHAME. ANSWER THE DOOR, ECK.

KNOCKITY-KNOCK!

HELLO — OOF!

MORNING! WE'RE FROM DESIGNER DECOR, INC. WE'VE COME TO DO YOUR DECORATING!

FIRST, TO SCRAPE OFF THE OLD PAPER — SWITCH ON THE STEAMER, CEDR — ER — FREDERICK!

HISS!

CLATTER! KLUNK!

And —

HOWL!

SHRIEK!

YELL!

SCRAPE!

SCRAPE!

OOH! YOU'RE SUPPOSED TO SCRAPE THE WALLPAPER — NOT OUR PANTS!

AWW!

OOYAH!

OOPS!

NOW FOR THE PAINT — SINCE YOU'RE JOCKS, WE THOUGHT YOU'D LIKE TARTAN PAINT!

DINNA BE DAFT. THERE'S NO SUCH THING!

TARTAN

TARTAN PAINT

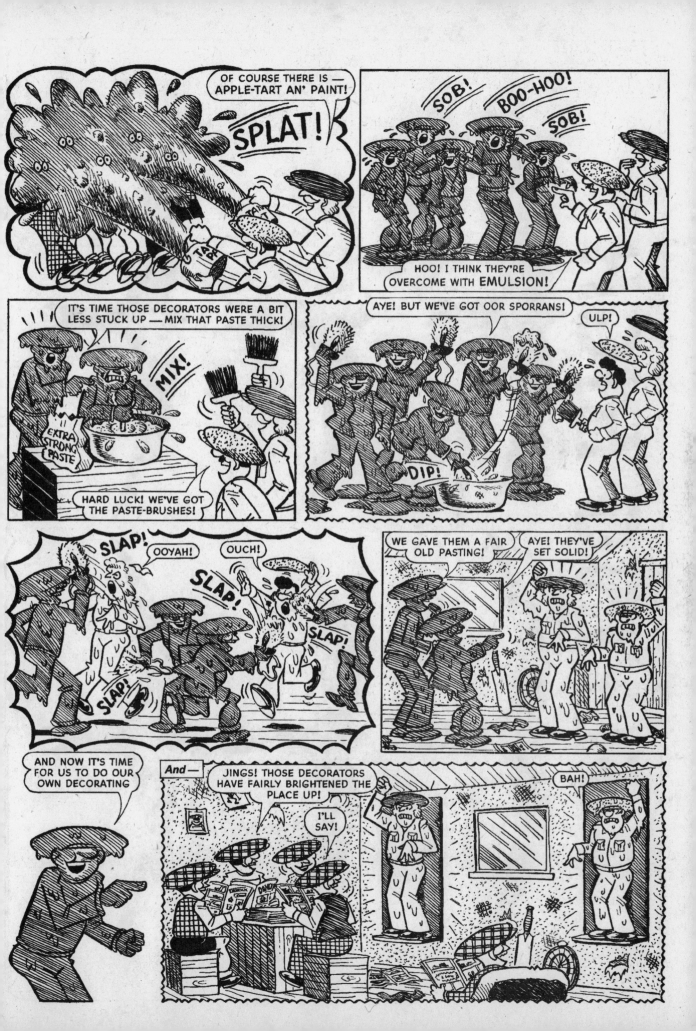

FLYING HIGH

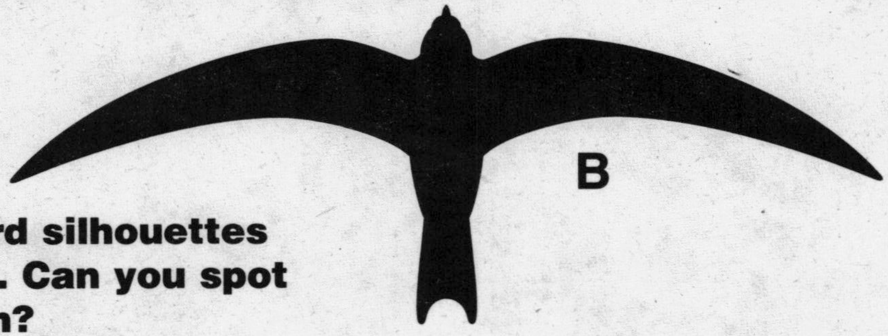

Two of these bird silhouettes are exactly alike. Can you spot them?

A

B

C

D

E

F

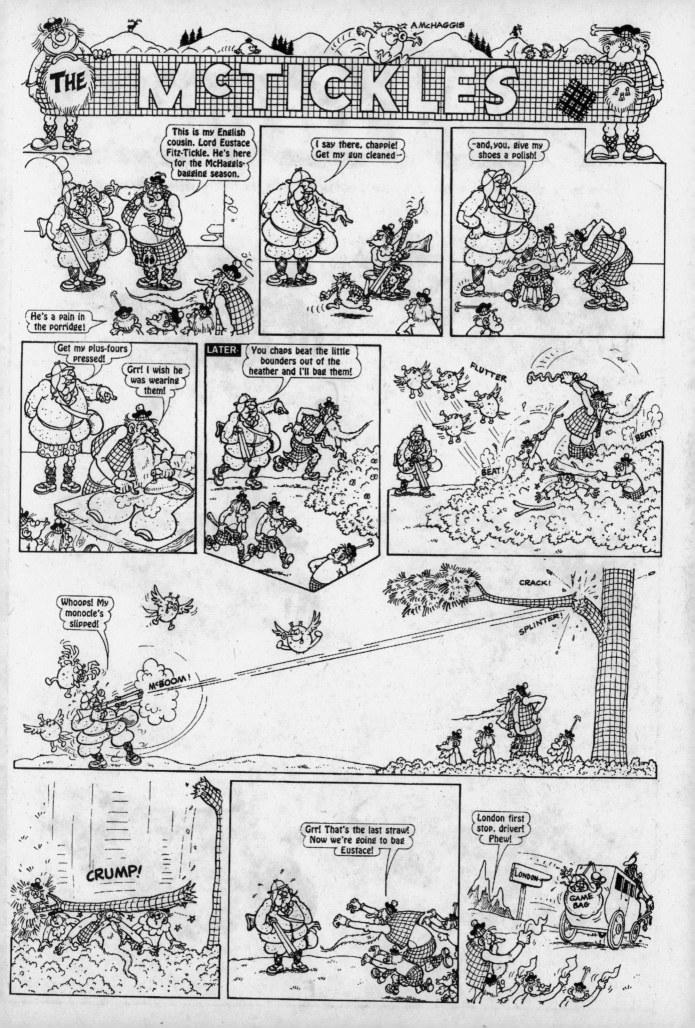

Don't Grouse

Only two of these black grouse pictures are exactly alike. Which two?

A

B

C

D

E

F

ANSWER: A, F

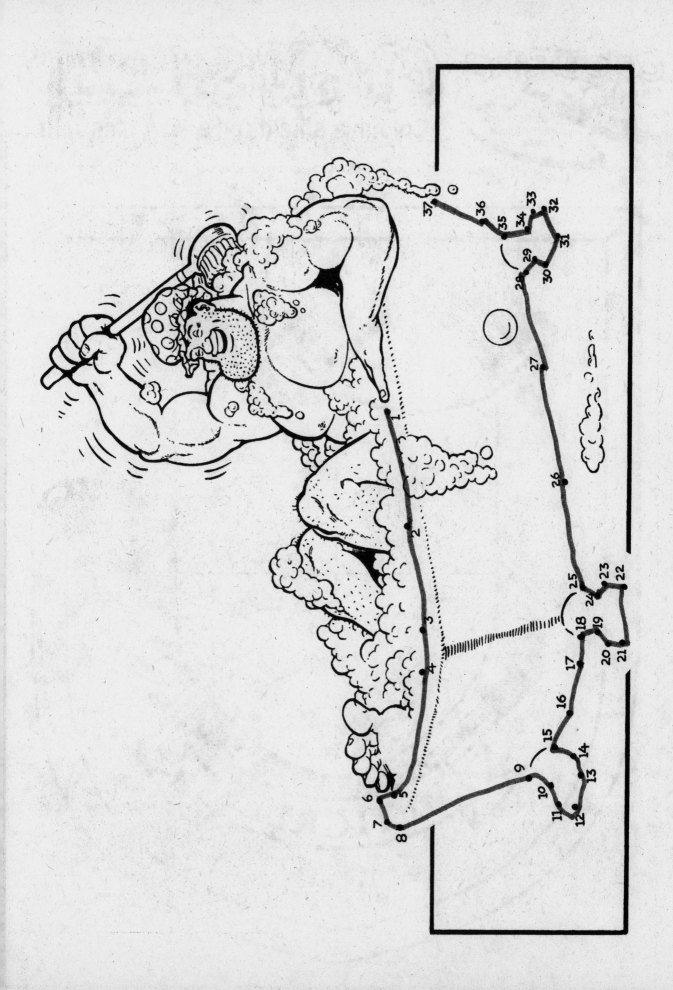

CLAN SHIELD

Colour a shield for a clan chieftain.

McTICKLES

HIDDEN name

HIDDEN name

Fill in the missing letters of the nine Scottish place names to reveal a Scottish tourist attraction in the shaded squares.

BANCHORY

LOCHABER

MONTROSE

STIRLING

ARISAIG

HIDDEN name

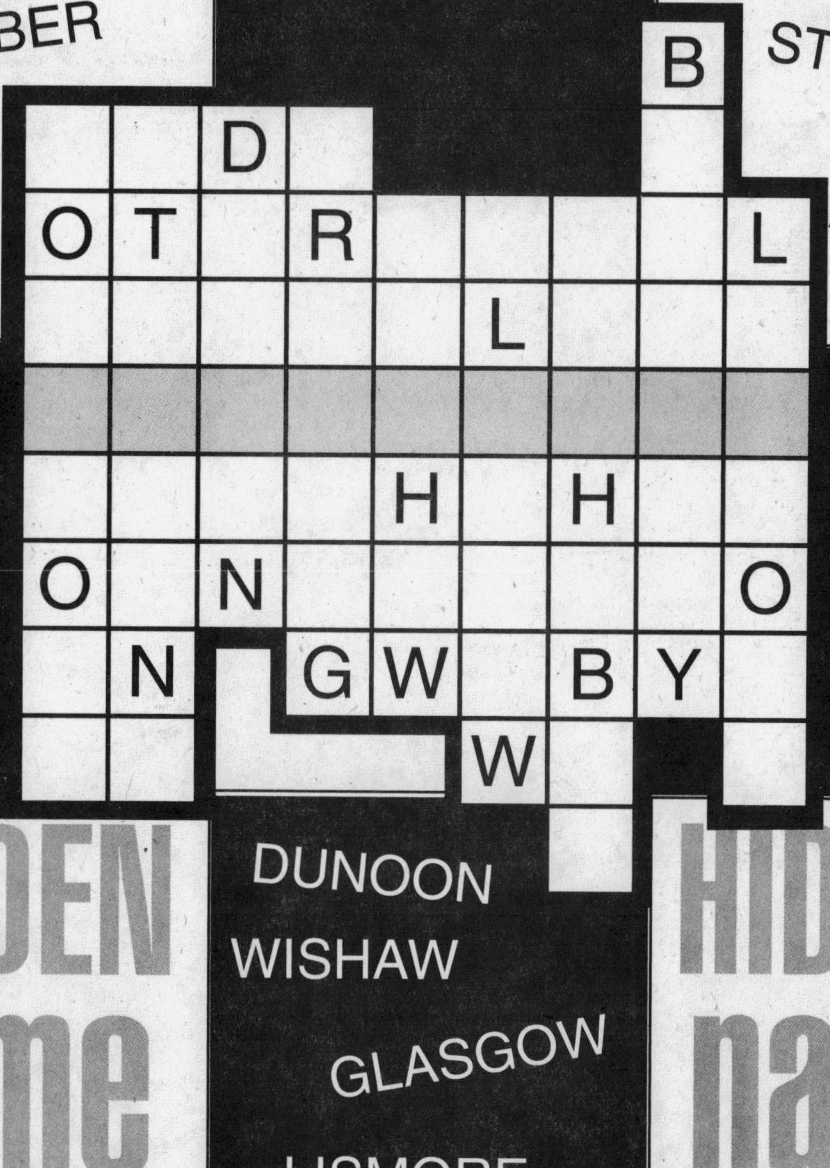

DUNOON

WISHAW

GLASGOW

LISMORE

HIDDEN name

ANSWERS

Montrose, Stirling, Dunoon, Arisaig, Wishaw, Glasgow, Lochaber, Banchory, Lismore. HIDDEN NAME :- Trossachs.

CLAWS FOR THOUGHT

Only three of these crabs are exactly alike.
Can you spot them?

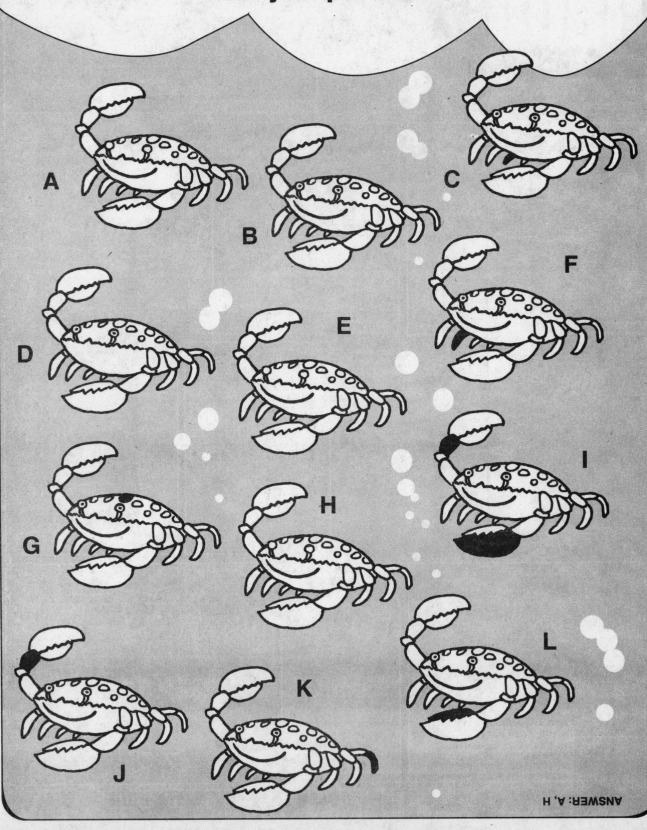

A

B

C

D

E

BEAT THE GOALIE

Which of these pictures is the odd-one-out?

F

G

H